To, David

Happy Christmas

GW00493065

FIT FOR
SWIMMING

Kelvin Juba

Foreword by
Adrian Moorhouse

PAVILION
MICHAEL JOSEPH

Published in association with The Sports Council

Acknowledgments

The author would like to thank David Hunt for his assistance with medical statistics, Keith Spain for the illustrations and Professor Clyde Williams for examining the scientific content. The Maxwell Swimming Pool at Aylesbury allowed us to photograph in their land conditioning area, Peter Presbury and Hatfield Swimming Club helped us and both Adrian Moorhouse and Robin Brew gave up their time to assist with this book.

To Sandy Webb: one of the funniest people I have met

First published in Great Britain in 1988 by
PAVILION BOOKS LIMITED
196 Shaftesbury Avenue, London WC2H 8JL
in association with Michael Joseph Limited
27 Wrights Lane, London W8 5TZ

British Library Cataloguing in Publication Data

Juba, Kelvin
  Fit for swimming. – (Fit for).
  1. Swimming
  I. Title
  797.2′1   GV837

  ISBN 1-85145-258-3

Printed and bound in Spain by Graficas Reunidas, Madrid

CONTENTS

Foreword

Introduction 1

1 Establishing Your Objectives 3

2 Before You Start 6

3 First Steps 12

4 Equipment 16

5 Land Conditioning 19

6 Avoiding Injury 26

7 Food and Drink 31

8 Joining a Club 45

9 Training Methods and Programmes 49

10 Getting Stronger 66

11 Keeping Records 77

12 The Big Day 80

Appendix 88

Index 90

FOREWORD

Swimming is one of the great, truly universal sports – a sport enjoyed throughout the world by millions of people. My own particular interest is in swimming at the very highest international level, but I recognize that most people are either not fortunate enough or simply don't want to compete at that level.

FIT FOR SWIMMING gives *everyone* the chance of joining in, whatever the level. You don't have to be an international swimmer to take part. However, the club, county or average swimmer can also benefit from this book which gives an insight into the wide range of training methods available in swimming. Furthermore it gives you a step by step guide on building and planning a training season.

Swimming used to be seen as a sport which appealed to the very young and the very young only. Slowly it has opened its doors to older age groups. It's gratifying to see the sport now appealing to not only the older competitive swimmers but also a wide range of people swimming purely for recreation and fitness. These people equally appreciate the precise nature of training structure and FIT FOR SWIMMING fills the ever widening gap in this particular market place. I'm therefore looking forward to seeing you all . . . down at the pool.

Adrian Moorhouse, M.B.E.
European Gold Medallist
Commonwealth Gold Medallist

INTRODUCTION

Swimming – The perfect exercise

In the distant past people learned to swim in order to be able to hunt, and hence survive. Later, soldiers were taught to swim, and it played an important part in warfare. Nowadays the reasons are different: we learn how to swim for the purposes of health and pleasure, and for use in emergencies.

In Britain more people are swimming than ever before. Figures produced by the Sports Council reveal that 3.2 million people in this country swim, including 30 per cent of people between the ages of 16 and 24 and 55 per cent of people between 25

June Croft, Olympic Bronze Medallist in the 400m Freestyle.

and 45. It's a popular misconception that swimming is for the young only. In fact, in the summer the actual number of swimmers swells to 4 million (17 per cent of adults).

Most people realize what good exercise swimming provides. As long as you can swim well, it is relatively injury-free compared to other sports. There are two main reasons for this: water resistance acts as a cushion, absorbing and smoothing out any jerky movements; and in the pool the proficient swimmer spends only a tiny proportion of the time in contact with the solid walls. The only real hazards are other swimmers. The result is that there is very little opportunity to jar ligaments and muscles. There are very few pulled muscles; cramp is generally the worst you can expect.

Swimming is a sport in which men and women can train and compete with equal proficiency. Also, although you won't be able to swim as fast as you get older, you can take a heavy training load for much longer than in almost any other activity because your body weight is partly offset by buoyancy.

Disabled people are also able to train and to get fit by swimming. It's a sport which reaches all parts of the body and involves all parts of the body in a way in which many sports don't.

Swimming is a great confidence developer. As with a child who is learning to read, this confidence can spread to other areas.

This book assumes that the reader already knows something of the stroke techniques and skills of swimming. It takes you from a situation in which, as with many people, you've been physically inert for a number of years and helps to sweep away the cobwebs in as painless a manner as possible. It shows you how to keep fit and how to prepare for a major event in your own personal calendar.

Equally, if you are already reasonably fit and want to remain fit, it gives you some further ideas on the sport.

There are many cogent arguments in favour of swimming as a way of achieving fitness and maintaining health, and hardly any against. It has rightly been called the perfect exercise.

1 ESTABLISHING YOUR OBJECTIVES

The most important factor in personal physical performance is to determine what you hope to achieve. It's quite likely that in due course you may have to reset your objectives following a process of personal evaluation, but establishing early goals will help to make your whole approach more purposeful.

In order to get the maximum out of your fitness programme, you need to determine your ultimate objective for each year and to work backwards in setting a programme to achieve that goal. Many people will just want to get fit, but this in itself can be made all the more interesting with a sense of direction. Here are some ideas for an ultimate goal in your training programme:

1) By competing in a national or local Masters competition (a Masters event allows for people over 25 years of age to compete at any age against people of a similar age as competitors are divided up into five-year age bands). Events for speed swimming exist for anything between 50 and 1,500 metres.

2) By targeting on distances rather than speed. For example, the Amateur Swimming Association (ASA) have a distance award scheme in which adults can even attempt a million yards should they wish.

3) By actually training for the purpose of entering long distance swimming races.

For the average swimmer, an annual goal would suffice. Many of us do not need a four-year programme, or the target of a major international games event to motivate us. Having determined what you want to go for, the next consideration should be how you are going to achieve this goal. For many people, self motivation becomes difficult when swimming after work on a cold dark winter's night. Training therefore becomes easier if a fairly rigid approach is adopted to the total training programme. Decide how many times a week you wish to train and try to establish a routine. There will always be unforeseen interruptions – illness, changes at work or extra demands from the family – so it will not always be possible to keep to it rigidly, but the odd missed session can usually be made up later.

For a person who is restarting swimming after a long period of inactivity, a typical outline programme might look like this:

Month	Length of sessions (hr)	Number of sessions per week	Distance to be swum
1	½	1	400m
2	½	2	800m
3	½	3	800m
4	¾	3	1500m
5	1	3	2000m
6	1	3	2500m
7	1	3	2700m
8	1	3	3000m
9	1½	3	3500m
10	1½	3	3700m
11	1½	3	4000m
12	1½	3	4500m

Whatever distances and lengths of session you choose, the important thing to bear in mind is the principle of steady progression.

You can measure your progress either by the distance swum or the time taken to do it. Don't imagine, however, that the best way of measuring it is by constantly swimming the same daily programme. There are many other factors governing performance, including your own physical and mental state as well as water conditions on a particular day. What will produce a more enthusiastic and, therefore, better performing swimmer is variety. A more constructive training programme, therefore, is a cyclical one, involving the repetition of one or two clearly identified sessions every three or four weeks.

The swimmer should try in the early months to lay a foundation of endurance on which speed can then be built. This can be achieved early on by reducing the length of rest between any repetitions. We all have a degree of organic fitness to go with muscle tone and our own inherent muscular composition. The swimmer's objective should be to stretch these variables.

Strength and, eventually, power and speed in the water can be added after a basic level of fitness has been reached. The real objective of people taking part in a swimming programme should be to get fitter and, in doing so, to improve their performance. An important part of your approach is to record in a log as much information as possible in order to evaluate your improvement. Whatever your age or level, measuring your performance is enjoyable and satisfying.

You should try to adopt an assertive approach to training, so that you always feel you are in control of your own training programme. Every so often, if your training programme is goal orientated, and has fully formulated objectives, you will need to reset those goals. Your mental approach towards your objective is therefore just as important at an early stage as it is when you are very fit.

2 BEFORE YOU START

Before committing yourself to a training programme, your first step should be to make sure that your body is healthy enough to be able to cope with the rigours of any form of training programme. If you smoke, then the efficiency of your lungs in swimming will be reduced. You will, therefore, need to stop smoking or gradually reduce the number of cigarettes you smoke until you give up. Alcohol should only be drunk in small amounts. One doesn't need to be fanatical about this but three pints of bitter every day is clearly going to be counter-productive.

You should also ask your doctor to measure your blood pressure. There are four main factors affecting normal blood pressure – cardiac output; peripheral resistance, or the resistance of the valve-like parts furthest away from the heart in the veins and arteries; viscosity of the blood and the elasticity of the arterial walls. These will all become important later on to a cardiac system which is called on to work hard.

The maximum pressure, known as systolic when the ventricles pump blood away from the heart, should be around 120mm of mercury (Hg) and the troughs in between, or diastolic pressure, should be around 80mm. The mean pressure would therefore be somewhere in the region of 100mm.

It's a useful idea to take your own resting pulse rate before starting the whole training programme. The usual resting heart rate of an adult human being is around seventy beats per minute. Those people in sedentary occupations will find that their heart rate is faster than that of trained athletes. The resting rate is probably most accurately taken immediately on waking in the morning before even getting out of bed. You take it by placing the hand over the heart and by counting the beats over a minute. This resting pulse rate can then be noted in your training log.

You should also get your doctor to test your lung capacity. In 1987 when the former Olympic swimming champion, David Wilkie, recommenced serious training, his doctor found that his lungs were only 65 per cent as efficient as they had been at his peak eleven years earlier. It can happen to the best of us!

Much of the early training of someone who is returning to training will be taken up by an endurance programme. The efficiency of the lungs is particularly important here. Oxygen consumption is the amount of oxygen supplied to your muscles and other tissues. It is measured by subtracting the amount of oxygen exhaled in one minute from the amount of oxygen inhaled.

We all have a maximal oxygen uptake or maximal oxygen consumption capacity (expressed as VO2 max.). This means the amount of oxygen that is consumed by the muscles in the course of activity. Women normally have a VO2 of two litres per minute, while that of men is about three litres. In both cases this can be increased

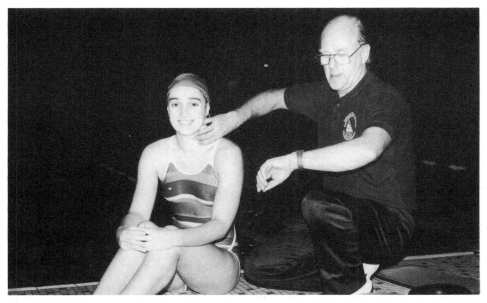

British Olympic Team and Hatfield Swimming Club Coach, Peter Presbury, works on pulse counts by applying pressure at the neck.

by up to a litre in well trained athletes.

It's therefore important to make sure that the lungs are working properly. Furthermore, this has a direct relationship to the weight and muscle/fat ratio in the body. A large person, particularly one who starts training when overweight, will use more oxygen per litre inhaled than someone who is smaller. This, in turn means a reduced swimming efficiency. Heredity can limit VO2, but it is still possible to improve it through training.

Weight is an important factor. You reach your optimum weight/strength ratio around the age of 18. Olof Lippold commented that as Masters swimmers get older, so they get heavier. It ought to be possible to use a simple formula which accounts for weight. The velocity (v) achieved by anyone's body moving through the water is ascertained by the square root of power (p), divided by displacement (m), multiplied by the constant which in turn is determined by body shape (k).

This can be simplifed as: $v = k/ \dfrac{p}{m}$

Lippold maintains that by using an extension of this formula, one can work out the times that can be achieved by simply losing weight. He cites himself as an example, stating that at 190 pounds, he has achieved 45 seconds for 50 metres breaststroke. He felt if he could lose 20 pounds in weight, the formula would look like this:

$T = 45/ \dfrac{170}{190} = 42.5$ sec.

He therefore concludes that, even if he did nothing else but lose weight, he could improve his 50 metre time by 2.5 seconds[1].

Your doctor will be able to advise on whether you are overweight. You may need to lose weight in order to be ready to start training. It's doubtful that you will lose more than a pound a day by training. You really need to reduce your daily calorie intake by eating gradually less. As with smoking, to train when you are overweight will be non-productive.

There is no accurate system for determining how much someone should weigh. For instance, the weight range of a fifteen-year-old can range over as much as 26

Acceptable Weight According to Height
(Note: height is without shoes, weight without clothes)

Height ft. in.	Men Weight (lb) Average	Men Weight (lb) Acceptable range	Women Weight (lb) Average	Women Weight (lb) Acceptable range
4 10			102	92-119
4 11			104	94-122
5 0			107	96-125
5 1			110	99-128
5 2	123	112-141	113	102-131
5 3	127	115-144	116	105-134
5 4	130	118-148	120	108-138
5 5	133	121-152	123	111-142
5 6	136	124-156	128	114-146
5 7	140	128-161	132	118-150
5 8	145	132-166	136	122-154
5 9	149	136-170	140	126-158
5 10	153	140-174	144	130-163
5 11	158	144-179	148	134-168
6 0	162	148-184	152	138-173
6 1	166	152-189		
6 2	171	156-194		
6 3	176	160-199		
6 4	181	164-204		

Source: Adapted from the recommendations of the Fogerty Centre Conference on Obesity, G. A. Bray (ed), Washington DC, National Institute of Health, 1979.

pounds. As a rough guide in the case of females, average acceptable weight is 100 pounds for the first five feet of height plus five pounds for each inch of height over five feet.

The relationship between your weight and your calorific needs during training will be important to you in the future. A person who weighs 110 pounds would require 1,872 calories for four hours of fast freestyle training (working at the rate of 240 min. × 7.8 calories per minute).

You have yet to determine the weight at which you will train most efficiently in the future. All you can do before you start training is to try to get down to an average weight – if you are overweight. Even more importantly, you will need to get your weight-body fat ratio into a reasonable balance. Surveys have shown that competitive male swimmers' ratio shows a fat composition of between 5 and 10 per cent of total body weight, whilst in females the range is from 14 to 26 per cent. If you can grab a handful of your skin fat, then you probably have between 15 and 20 per cent as a ratio if you are a man, and between 25 and 30 per cent if you are a woman.

For those people who are about to start training but who are too heavy, the next stage is obviously to lose some weight. How fast can you realistically expect to lose weight if you are going to commence training at more or less the same time? A very rapid weight loss is not even desirable, because it is normally due chiefly to water and muscle wasting. A slower weight loss avoids this and produces a greater loss of fat weight. You will know if you are losing too much weight through water loss because you will dehydrate. This manifests itself in grogginess and muscle cramps.

If you lose one or two pounds of fat per week, you will maximize fat loss. Incidentally, one pound of fat in your body represents 3,500 calories that either you eat or your body uses. That is a fair amount of energy to lose by training and it means having to eat 3,500 calories less a day just to lose one pound. Let's imagine you are a little overweight before you turn to the water. You may find it a struggle to get used to eating just 1,500 calories a day.

The best approach might be to go through a light dry land exercise programme at home in which you subject your body to regular rhythmic exercise of a medium intensity. This intensity means that you will be working at about 70 per cent of your maximum heart rate. By doing this, there is a tendency for your body to use more fat as a fuel source, which preserves the limited glycogen which you may have at this stage. Glycogen comes from eating carbohydrates.

One ounce of fat contains some 219 calories; the same quantity of carbohydrate contains 112, protein 112, and alcohol 196. It's easy to see that reducing fat alone will help. Here are some ideas on how you can keep an eye on your weight either before or just as you are about to start training:

1 Eat and digest food slowly.

2 Avoid fatty foods or foods with hidden fats, sugar and added fats.

3 Resist quick weight loss diets and go for a steady weight loss.

4 Eat three or four meals or snacks a day instead of big meals.

5 Boiled or steamed foods or alternatively fresh foods are preferable to fried meals.

6 High nutrient density foods should be eaten such as vegetables, fruits, lean meats, low fat dairy produce.

Your fat weight not only includes visible fat but fat stored in the adipose tissue in your body weight. It is usually measured from your body skinfolds, although there can be as much as a 5 per cent error in estimating this. The skinfolds are measured by means of calipers.

Although it is known that fat makes up 26 per cent of the average adult female and 15 per cent of the male[2], what no one knows is what the optimum proportions are. It will therefore be difficult for your doctor to be wholly accurate, but he may be able to give you a rough guide.

3 FIRST STEPS

Working your way back to fitness can often be a painful experience. Those people who are already swimming once a week and want to step up their training programme are going to find it very much easier. Fortunately, many swimming pools have a lane set aside for those people who want to swim lengths. They're normally given names such as 'jogging' lanes. Usually they consist of adults or fitness swimmers who are swimming lengths at reasonable speeds. These lanes are normally available at lunch time or in the early part of the evening. It's probably here where you might start.

Having a partner of approximately the same ability to compete against will help, but the partner will need to be fully committed. A partner attending irregularly could be more of a hindrance than a help. There are very few people who are fortunate enough to be able to find a local Masters swimming club with whom to train. Occasionally you come across incentive schemes which may help to get you off the mark. For instance, the Guild of London Baths Managers hold a London Swim-

Training in groups can be great fun. This photograph shows a training group working together.

arathon every year in conjunction with the South East Region of the Sports Council. Swimmers can compete or swim for fun over 2,500 or 5,000 metres. Similar campaigns have been held in other places such as Leeds and York. The most important factor behind these campaigns is the encouragement of people to train in order to be ready to take part. Many pools are designed purely as leisure or fun pools, and unless they have a 25 metre swimming area (and some of them do), these wouldn't be very beneficial to the fitness swimmer.

Try to find a pool of 25 metres or more which is not too busy. You can derive benefit in any length of pool, but 25 metres will allow you to get into a steady rhythm where you can gradually overload the body systems. Furthermore, you can monitor your early stroke cadence through stroke counting, more easily in a longer pool. Don't waste time with a pool where lengths are not going to be encouraged. It's my contention that every non-leisure pool should allocate at least one roped off lane an hour every day for fitness. Pools with a separate diving well are always going to be easier for the fitness swimmer because they result in less interruptions due to people diving out in front of you whilst swimming lengths.

How then should you approach the first stages? The session would need to start with two or three minutes of stretching exercises, mainly concentrating on loosening the shoulders and ankles. Some suggested exercises are to be found in later chapters. On entering the pool, the swimmer will need to approach the first few sessions gradually. Plenty of variety in training is the key. During the first week, concentrate mainly on completing lengths, using your first (preferred) stroke. Try to make everything as economic as possible. For instance, you might swim 50 metre repetitions, with a minute between each repetition, aiming to complete the distance in fifty seconds. You should try to hold the same number of strokes – perhaps forty strokes – for each 50 metre swim.

In the first session, you might include five of these repetitions. During the next session, you might repeat this aiming to hold the same number of strokes while lowering your time to 48 seconds. This could mean that each stroke has become more powerful.

During the first two weeks, you really need to make at least one long, steady swim, concentrating on technique. Go for a steady approach in which you try to make each pull correct under the water. Many people will not have the benefit of a swimming teacher to correct them; but if it feels good, and you are not splashing recovering your arms, you are probably on the right track.

By the end of the first week, you will have developed an initial basis from which to work. Your training sessions now need to be constructed so that they have a regular pattern which suits you. They could be constructed as follows:

To Build up Legs

Allocation of		Item
Time (min.)	Distance (m)	
4	200	Warm up – 2nd stroke
8	400	Hard swim – 1st stroke
12	400	Series of repetitions – 1st/2nd stroke
6	200	Series of repetitions – kicking on opposite stroke (i.e. 2nd/1st stroke)
4	200	A few sprints
34	1,400	

To Build up Arms

Allocation of		Item
Time (min.)	Distance (m)	
4	8 × 25	Medium pace warm up swims – 1st stroke
8	600	Hard swim – 2nd stroke
10	6 × 100	Series of repetitions – arms only – 1st stroke
8	400	Alternating lengths of full stroke and legs
4	6 × 25	Sprints in individual medley order
34	1,950	

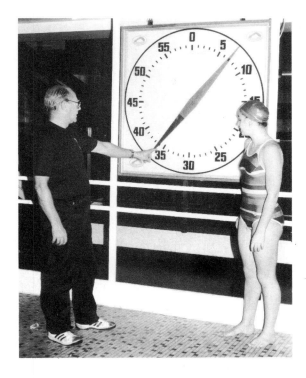

The value of a clearly displayed and seen pace clock is enormous. Here, Peter Presbury runs through anticipated split times in a swim about to be made.

It's important to get into some other good habits at this early stage. Most pools have a large clock. Try to use it, and to set off each time with the second hand at twelve. It makes it easier to remember your times at the end of a swim.

After one or two of these swims take your pulse count and record it in your log for future reference. Pulse counting provides a good indication of general fitness. It tells you how fast the heart is working in order to achieve a certain work level. What it doesn't tell you is how efficiently it is working. At this early stage, your heart will pump faster to reach certain levels of speed.

The pulse can be taken by pressing the middle finger either directly on to the heart or on to the carotid artery along the side of the head three centimetres beneath the base of the ear lobe. It can also be taken by pressing the middle finger of the extended hand on to the centre of the inside of the wrist. These pulse checks can be taken for fifteen seconds and multiplied by four to get a reading for a minute.

4 EQUIPMENT

Swimming is a low cost sport. Unlike many sports, it requires very little equipment, and much of it is quite cheap by comparison with the likes of golf or skiing.

The swimming costume is obviously the most important piece of equipment. It needs to be close fitting, whether for men or women, so that it doesn't trap water or air and these days most costumes are now made of lycra, a lightweight material that avoids drag and resistance. Both woollen swimsuits and the boxer shorts style of costume will not be an aid; nor are women's two-piece swimsuits recommended, as they tend to make shoulder movement in the water more difficult. A costume that finishes close to the neck is preferable. One problem with women's swimwear is that it changes with fashion; another is that it can be damaged by sea salt, sand and sun tanning oils if you use it as a multi-purpose suit, and the new lightweight materials tend to ladder if rubbed against abrasive surfaces. Both men's and women's costumes need to be rinsed in tap water after swimming because chlorine in water can cause them to rot. Most manufacturers provide instructions for drying the suits. The best advice in the end is probably just to wear what feels good and suits you.

With women's swimwear, it's a good idea to check carefully the stitching on the inside of straps, as a tough thread may rub during continuous arm movements and cause shoulder burns. There ought to be a reasonable amount of free movement in both arms and legs, so that you can lift the shoulder straps by about five centimetres. If you particularly like a costume for other reasons, but it rubs slightly, then apply petroleum jelly to the area.

It's always a good idea to take a second costume in your bag when you go training. You can't go far wrong by purchasing either Speedo or Arena swimwear, the average

16

prices being around £9–10 for women's costumes and £4–5 for men's. Specialist swimming shops tend to have a greater variety and are often cheaper than the ordinary sports shop (addresses can be found in *Swimming Times*).

There are many brands of goggles now available. Most of them are of the light-weight variety. In some cases the plastic eye pieces tend to mist up. This can be avoided by either licking the inside before putting them on, or alternatively by pur-chasing 'Anti-Fog' goggles which do not mist up. If you are returning to swimming after a number of years and haven't used lightweight goggles before, great care should be taken when putting them on and taking them off. The strong elasticated support which goes around the back of the head can create problems. Never put the elasticated part on first, separately, because when you put the eye pieces on they can spring back into the eyes. Keeping it in one piece, loop the elasticated part round the back of the head and then slide the eye pieces over the eyes.

Goggles can also let in water or slip off. This can be overcome by firmly pressing the rims of the goggles against the bones surrounding the eyes, so that there is a fair degree of suction. Goggles are normally priced from £3.

There is a range of additional equipment which you might consider to be optional to your kit bag. Handle paddles can be useful early on. The effect of them is to over-load the arms during pulling by creating extra resistance, and they also help you to ensure that the arms are aligned carefully during the pull.

Flippers can be used for legs-only work. They tend to dislocate full stroke techni-que, but help to both loosen up and overload the ankles on alternating techniques. However, you will also need to practise without flippers. When the flippers are taken off, a drop in the leg position will come about and the levers shorten, so that slightly different sets of muscles are used.

Always keep a float in your kit bag. Polystyrene floats are generally used. A large float made of foam polystyrene is the best for adults and helps to get the body into the right kicking position.

Drag suits are still used as a training device. These are specially designed cos-tumes made of heavier material and with pockets positioned so as to catch water as it travels past the body. They provide variety in training. Some swimmers even train with divers' weight belts to increase resistance. Arms-only work can be practised in two ways, either with a pull buoy or with a rubber band. The band, which can be a section from a car tyre, needs to be about three inches in width and big enough to go round both legs at the ankles. The band is cheap and effective, but tends to make the legs very low in the water on freestyle and backstroke.

The pull buoy, on the other hand, which is made of two cylindrical pieces of polystyrene held together with two adjoining lengths of rope, tends to lift the feet high and close to the surface. The pull buoy is used by placing it between the legs generally above the knees but it can be used even between the ankles.

There are other training devices on the market, often from America, but many are not all that practical for normal training. It's even possible to get a device which loops around the upper head and plays music in order to alleviate boredom during training programmes.

Table of Swimming Equipment Optional Extras		
Item	**From**	**Approx. cost ($)**
Hand paddles	Swimming specialist retailer	2-4
Flippers	Sports retailer	9-11
Towels	Sports/household retailer	4-5
Latex swim caps	Sports retailer	1
Expanded polystyrene swim floats	Sports/swimming retailer	4-5
Pull buoy (leg floats)	Swimming specialist retailer	1-2
Rubber tyre section	Homemade/garage	0
Drag suits	Mail order	15
Earplugs	Chemist/sports retailer	2-3
Noseclips	Direct from 'Laxto'	2

5 LAND CONDITIONING

Whilst getting fit, one should treat the land conditioning work as secondary, playing a supporting role. During the first few weeks, you may just feel too tired from training in the water and some light flexibility work may be enough.

The land work, which should be tailored to the particular needs of each individual, should be as specific as possible. During the early stages, a great amount of flexibility work is needed, especially if you haven't swum for a while. Strength training and training designed to increase power can come later as the training load is

Robin Brew, 1984 Olympic Record Holder in the 200 metres Individual Medley as well as The BBC Television Super Stars Champion, demonstrates the all round strength which has resulted in his becoming one of the world's leading tri-athletes. Here we see power developed through the use of multi gym equipment.

Latissimus Pulls. Position pull a maximum weight, from a position where the arms are outstretched above, by bending the elbows. The bar is pulled to the back of the neck.

Upright Rowing. The bar starts at arm's length reach, by the legs. It is then pulled to the chin by bending the elbows and bringing the triceps muscles into play.

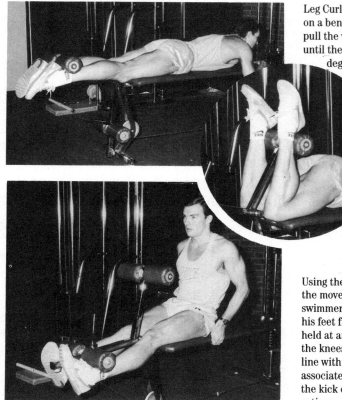

Leg Curls. Whilst the swimmer lies flat on a bench, the knees are bent so as to pull the weight in a circular action until the feet are at an angle of 45 degrees, above the knees. A good exercise for backstroke leg recovery.

Using the same piece of equipment the movement is reversed. The swimmer, whilst sitting, merely lifts his feet from a point where they are held at an angle of 45 degrees below the knees until the feet are almost in line with the hips. This exercise is associated with the leg extension and the kick of all up and down leg actions.

steadily increased.

General endurance can be developed in the water. If, however, you find it difficult to get to the pool or there isn't any opportunity for swimming lengths at your pool, then some limited running or circuit training would help. However, running does tend to harden muscles in the lower leg and ankles, an area where one is looking for increased looseness.

As a general guide, five minutes should be spent at the poolside before each training session concentrating on flexibility, and the amount of time devoted to land conditioning each week should be equivalent to approximately 20 per cent of that spent in the swimming pool.

20

This exercise allows the rotation of hands and forearms inwards and together in front of the face.

Bench Press. A powerful extension of the elbows is required for this exercise whilst keeping the upper body firmly on the bench.

As you get older, most joints stiffen and mobility is lost. In swimming this applies particularly to the ankle region. It is for this reason that many adults learning to swim do so on breast-stroke which, although possibly the most complex of the four strokes in mechanical terms, makes fewer demands on the ankles. By comparison, young children tend to learn on dog paddle or backstroke.

If you are planning to swim strokes other than breast-stroke, the ankle mobility work is vital. The hip joint is also important on all strokes in both flexion and extension in order to provide the first lever for the kick and to bring in the large muscles of the upper leg. However, the hip region is more difficult to work on than the ankles.

Flexibility in the ankles manifests itself in three ways. First, in the form of plan-

Whilst seated, the swimmer extends the elbows so that the weight is pressed fully above the head. This is a good all round exercise with which to start a session.

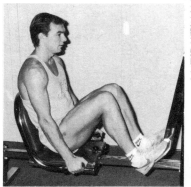

Leg Exercises. This is an exercise closely associated with the breast-stroke kick, starts and turns. The swimmer aims to push with the feet until the knees are fully extended.

tar flexion, i.e. with the toes pointed; secondly, in the 'toe in' at the ankles produced by the inward rotation of the legs at the knees; thirdly, in the tightening of the ankle region which is produced by curling the toes and which is useful in breast-stroke.

In your loosening-up before entering the water, try some simple ankle circling exercises. Whilst sitting, hold the left ankle so that the heel is controlled in your right hand and the front of the foot is held from underneath in your left hand. Keeping the heel steady, circle the foot as widely as possible in one direction and after thirty seconds, rotate in the opposite direction. Then change hands and feet.

 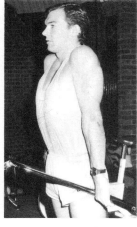

The Shrug. After holding the weight securely at full arm extension, the swimmer raises his shoulders by shrugging them towards his ears. This exercise assimilates the first part of the arm recovery in most strokes.

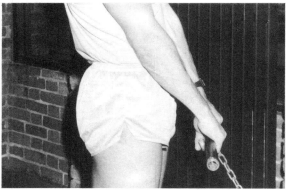 

Triceps Curls. The swimmer wraps his hands over the bar starting from an extended position, he pulls the weight in a semi circular movement until it reaches the chin. The hands should be wrapped *over* the bar.

In another exercise the ankle and hip regions can be worked together. Stand on the side of the pool with your body upright. Hold one ankle in the corresponding hand. Bend the knees in a breast-stroke-like movement and try to bring the curled foot up towards, and slightly in front of, the hips. Apply gentle pressure and then repeat with the other foot. Hyperextension of the ankle can then be improved by another knee-bending exercise, this time lifting the ankle behind you and placing the sole of the foot against the small of the back. Then change to the other foot.

These are all quite simple exercises which can be done on the poolside or at

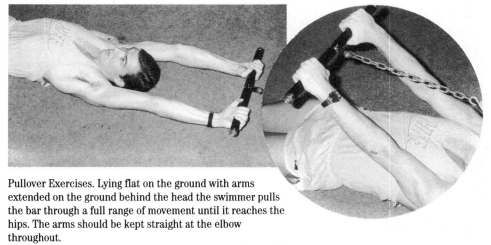

Pullover Exercises. Lying flat on the ground with arms extended on the ground behind the head the swimmer pulls the bar through a full range of movement until it reaches the hips. The arms should be kept straight at the elbow throughout.

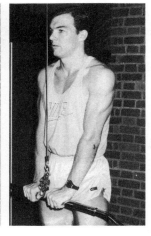

Low Triceps Curl. From a standing position, the swimmer is able to complete the first phase of the curl using the lower start position to bring other muscles into play.

home and which will help to create greater flexibility. They can be used either to help prevent simple strains or to cure muscular pains such as cramp.

Now lie flat on your back with your arms by your sides. Point your toes and aim to get your soles to lie flat on the floor. Then point your toes and rotate the knees inwards so that the ankles toe in. Follow this by remaining on your back and attempting to swing one foot at a time to place the toe of that foot on the ground in parallel with that shoulder whilst keeping the leg straight at the knees.

Sit Ups with Twist. The stomach and trunk, used mostly for balance and body position, is a difficult area to isolate in strengthening movements. Nevertheless most multi gyms have units for this exercise. The swimmer leads with alternating elbows in sitting up from a point where he has been lying diagonally on the bench. This has the advantage of strengthening a greater area of the stomach region.

Stretch cords used as pulleys and mounted to a wall can be advantageous to both local endurance in the shoulder region and to arm strength in pulling movements.

The shoulders are a third important area for mobilization. Keeping the body upright, circle one arm slowly by swinging the hand through a 360-degree circle. Speed can be varied and the arm then swung in the opposite direction. You can then change arms, again varying the direction and trying to keep the arm up against your ear. Now swing both arms backwards together. Do it quickly at first, but after 15 seconds slow the movement down so that the head is pushed well out in front of the shoulders and the shoulder blades feel as though they are going to scrape together.

Now bend your body forward at the hips through a 45-degree angle and go through the alternating freestyle movement with the arms. This can be followed by simulating the butterfly arm recovery with your eyes fixed on the ground.

There are many other exercises, shown on p.69 in diagrammatic form, all of which can be done on the poolside. It is not worth trying anything more complicated at this stage, as you could end up with muscular pains.

If you find it difficult to get to a local pool, jogging can be of some value to the respiratory system, but the benefits are small and generally the exercise isn't specific to swimming. The action of running itself has a greater overload effect than that of swimming because the effect of carrying your own weight as well as exercising means a greater effort has to be made to retain a reasonable level of performance.

The three most common problems at the start come about through the body's muscles being asked to cope with a situation that is new:

1. Cramp can occur in the legs, particularly when pushing off from a pool wall or when changing leg actions from breast-stroke to butterfly or an alternating movement and vice versa. It has come about because of a sharp contraction of the flexors, and can be overcome by extending the muscles lightly where the cramp is centred. One method with leg cramp is to sit on the poolside with your legs straight, grasping your toes and curling them backwards. If that fails, try warming the area, either by standing under a hot shower, or by drying the area with a towel until it is warm.

2. Continual use of the shoulder region in a rotational movement leads to a condition known as tendonitis; but this is only likely to happen if the swimmer completes large distances. There are a number of cures, ranging from a simple rub to freezing the area or having a cortizone injection. Probably the best advice is to prevent it from happening by easing back on the distances you swim in the early stages.

3. Stitch is a problem which all swimmers, even the fittest, have to overcome from time to time. It occurs in the form of stomach cramp when you are working hard. There is no way of avoiding it because stitch occurs at any time.

The only way of counteracting it is to ease back slightly. Continuing to swim at a steadier pace has much the same effect as stopping to wait for it to ease.

6 AVOIDING INJURY

In the previous chapter, I suggested some very simple exercises which would assist with early stretching and mobility and as a consequence help to prevent injury. In fact there are very few people who suffer injuries in swimming, largely because it isn't a contact sport. The only impact with solid objects occurs during the relatively short span of wall contact on starts and turns.

It follows that the more likely areas for concern are illness, damage to the body through repetition of movements and problems brought about by the effects of water on eyes, ears and nose.

The cornerstones of avoiding injury early on are:

a) a warm-up session consisting of a variety of stretching exercises and a warm-up in the water.

b) drying down fully and wrapping correctly after a swim on a cold winter's night. Headwear is vital.

c) drying the ears fully at the end of a session.

d) a steady, progressive approach to training.

However, problems may still occur and these are most likely to be in the following areas: shoulder region; breast-stroker's knee; eyes, ears and nose; anaemic problems; effects of smoking and drinking.

Shoulder region All swimming strokes call for continuous rotation of this joint, which has a ball and socket structure. There is little ligamentous restraint. Most problems occur because of either overstress or incorrect technique. Unless you have a coach or training partner to point out faults, incorrect technique is going to be hard to overcome.

Common technical faults bring the following problems:

Stroke	Fault	Muscle of shoulder region
Freestyle	Arm recovery	Anterior deltoid
Freestyle	Dropped elbow	Middle deltoid
Freestyle	Lifting arm on recovery	Posterior deltoid
Butterfly	Arm recovery	Anterior deltoid
Butterfly	Dropped elbow	Middle deltoid
Butterfly	Lifting arm on recovery	Posterior deltoid
Breast-stroke	Arm recovery	Anterior deltoid
Backstroke	First part of recovery	Posterior deltoid

The most common shoulder problem for swimmers is tendonitis or inflammation of the shoulder. It comes about because the shoulder has been slightly strained and hasn't been given time to rehabilitate[3]. Aronen maintained that with the tendons not adequately stabilized, they can become inflamed by impingement with ligaments or bones. He felt that at two degrees, a gradual onset of inflammation occurred, particularly in movements when the arms were over the head. He described the fact that swimmers need to 'milk' the swelling out of the inflamed tendon with repeated impingement of the inflamed tendon by easy movement. Failing this, rest is important and, failing that, medication. Early in your training programme, rest should be sufficient. Tendonitis, however, tends to build on a muscular problem already in existence. The result is often secondary pain where initiation occurs at the long head of the biceps.

A lower degree of tendonitis (i.e. one degree) comes about where the tendon comes away from its groove. How can the swimmer deal with this potentially regular problem? Rest is the first cure, though this can be annoying to keen swimmers who have recently returned to training. Another is to keep the arm in a sling, which takes the weight off the arm and shoulder. If these have no effect, applying ice packs in the area for twenty minutes after each swim will help decrease inflammation.

When the shoulder has had sufficient rest, some strengthening on land will help to decrease inflammation. Your doctor could probably offer advice, but you have to bear in mind that their main concern is with people not suffering from self-inflicted injuries and illnesses. Very few GPs have much knowledge of the special conditions of swimming training. Chapter 10 describes ways of improving shoulder region strength through the use of resistance pulleys.

Breast-stroker's knee Most people who swim breast-stroke know how painful this can be. The medial menscus and collateral ligaments, which lie around the knee, inflame. This comes about by swimmers trying to kick and rotate their legs outwards, which is not really a natural movement for the human knee structure. This can be avoided by using a narrower leg action, in other words by kicking with the feet closer together. You will lose something in terms of propulsion because there is more drag associated with kicking the feet directly backwards. This may be worth losing at the first twitches of pain.

Breast-stroker's knee is best avoided by simply swimming less breast-stroke in training. Not more than 40 per cent of the training session should consist of breast-stroke. As always, prevention is better than cure, and here a steady build-up over the weeks is needed.

Eyes Before the introduction of the lightweight goggle, there were continual problems for many swimmers who had their heads immersed in water whilst training over long periods. Thankfully, many of these problems have been eradicated with the use of goggles, some of which are tinted to cut out sunlight. Difficulties arise where the pH of the water (the acid-alkaline content) is much greater or smaller than 7.4, which is the condition closest to water in the eye. The conjunctiva becomes irritated and this gets worse in warm water or bright sunlight. Goggles are really the best preventative. However, if you have difficulty in wearing goggles, an eye cup of salt in water solution before training may help.

Pink or red eye will come about if the cornea is rubbed. The cornea fills with water, which can produce swelling. It can lose some of its cells on the surface and the eye becomes worse. One word of warning about goggles – it is better not to wear someone else's. Adeno virus type 3, the only transmittable eye infection, can be passed on in this way.

Ears The ears are another problem area. Drying the ears thoroughly after swimming can help. Regular ear sufferers can use acetic acid or a cotton wool stick of cortisporin otic suspension to prevent ear infection. If this fails, long periods of rest from the water are advisable. Sometimes, getting soap or shampoo or water directly in the ear during a shower after training can create ear trouble.

Swimmers preparing for long distance races may need to take a protective shield of baby or olive oil. Swimming regularly in open water causes a thickening of bone in the middle ear, known as exostosis, and the use of oil can help to avoid this.

Otitis external is the most common infection in swimmers. When excess water is left in the ear, it slowly works its way out but leaves debris in the external auditory canal. Warm, moist conditions encourage the infection, and if the ear is attacked by bacteria or fungus, the debris will be used as food. This causes greater swelling and can produce pus.

Anaemia Anaemia tends to affect women in particular, but it can also harm men. It comes about through iron deficiency and a reduction in haemoglobin content in the red blood cells. These cells transport oxygen to and from the muscles, as well as in the muscles themselves. A lack of iron therefore has a direct relationship with endurance. The recommended daily amount of iron is 12 milligrams for men and 18 for women. A normal diet contains six of these for every 1,000 calories[4]. In order to keep up a reasonable training programme, you will be taking between 3,000 and 5,000 calories per day, as I will relate later. Your daily requirement of iron should therefore be covered. To be on the safe side, try to eat eggs, leafy vegetables, watercress and dried fruits when embarking on your training programme.

There can also be anaemia-related problems if there is an attempt to lose too much weight when starting a new training programme. Some fat, essential fat, is needed for energy, and the minimum amount of tolerable thinness is likely to be related to hereditary factors. When weight reduction is taken to extremes and the level of fat drops below 15 per cent, women can suffer amenorrhea[5] or lack of menstruation.

Smoking and drinking These don't really mix with a stringent training programme. Drinking alcohol in moderation shouldn't be a problem, but regular high levels of alcohol increase the chance of mineral and vitamin deficiencies. Liver and brain cells[6] die each time they come into contact with alcohol. Liver cells can be replaced, but those of the brain can't.

So far, some research has shown that drinking small amounts of alcohol before exercising may be ergocentric. Performance would be limited by inhibition of physiological factors linked to this. Blood alcohol levels of 0.4 and 0.6[6] have produced large decreases in reaction time, eye-hand co-ordination, balance, complex co-ordination and visual tracking. Drinking small amounts of alcohol and then exercising has very little effect on heart, lungs and metabolism, even if it's a maximum effort or if it's a matter of strength or endurance.

Smoking can be much more of a problem. Vital capacity can be seriously reduced, as can respiratory flow, and smoking will dramatically affect your training and racing performance. Don't inflict injury on yourself!

Massage could have a part to play in avoiding further injury and there are many physiotherapists and masseurs specializing in sports injuries. Essentially massage can smoothe the nervous system as well as stimulate the flow of blood and lymph. It has a third role of easing pain and healing the injured part. By doing so it can remove lactic acid build-up which often results from unaccustomed exercise. A massage cannot help if a haematone or tearing injury has occurred. In this case ice and rest are the first stages. This will probably mean not doing anything about it for 48 hours. Ice dulls pain and reduces swellings. Massage can help with both tendonitis and breast-stroker's knee.

Nevertheless, swimming remains a sport where very few injuries occur. Dr D Hunt, a member of the ASA's Scientific Committee, recently carried out a study of swimmers at Clay Cross in Derbyshire over a six-month period. He found that the swimmers as a group were completing four hundred swimming hours per week. This meant a total of 10,400 hours over 26 weeks. In that time only ten swimming injuries occurred – or one injury every 1,040 hours.

7 FOOD AND DRINK

Like any other machine, the body needs to be constantly refuelled, and this needs to be carried out with suitable refuelling. Diet is therefore a most important area, but it can be overemphasized. So much is written about the subject that it is difficult to be helpful without being controversial.

The factors governing diet are availability of types of food, economics and our ability to detect our needs. These govern how our bodies will take in vitamins, fats, proteins, minerals, water and carbohydrates – our bodies' main needs. Carbohydrates are important to us as a source of energy for muscular contraction, mainly through the use of sugar. Fats are a further source of energy and can be stored for occasions when sugar has to be conserved for further energy needs. Proteins are used for growth and repair, but can be called on for energy when fats and carbohydrates are no longer in evidence.

The National Advisory Committee on Nutrition Education recommend that the proportions of food intake should be 50 per cent carbohydrates, 30 per cent fats and 20 per cent proteins for the average adult. They also recommend a 5 per cent higher fat intake in adolescents to the age of 18. After that fats can be increased from 25 to 30 per cent.

However, swimmers now compete with a recommended breakdown of 70–75 per cent carbohydrates, 10–15 per cent fats, 15–20 per cent protein according to Maglischo[7]. For all serious swimmers, a basic knowledge of the dietary system is helpful in determining their foods. Loughborough University have also found in tests on their top athletes that they perform at their best on a 15 per cent intake of protein. Good diet is essential to swimmers, as swimming takes up four times as much energy as running the same distance.

For the purposes of someone embarking on a serious training programme, the dietary requirements may be expressed as:

	Sprint Swimming	Endurance Swimming
1st requirement	carbohydrates ⟶ simple sugars	carbohydrates ⟶ simple sugars
2nd requirement	Proteins ⟶ amino acids ⟶ Urea	Fats ⟶ fatty acids + glycerol
3rd requirement		Proteins ⟶ amino acids ⟶ Urea
	↓	↓
	glucose ⟶ energy ⟶ fat ⟶ liver/muscle glycogen	glucose ⟶ energy ⟶ fat ⟶ liver/muscle glycogen

Although one needs to eat a well balanced diet, carbohydrate is important to a regular training programme. Chemical reactions take place in the stomach and small intestine by which the three major categories of food are broken down, absorbed through the stomach wall and held for use in various parts of the body when needed.

For example, carbohydrate becomes glycogen or simple sugars. They are stored in this form in the liver and muscle fibres. Some of the sugars are converted to fat and the body creates its own form of storage by creating fat in this way.

In the secondary category, fatty acids and glycerol are ready for use as a later fuel source. These, like some carbohydrate parts, are held on a temporary basis ready for use in the muscle fibres, whilst the balance is kept as fat around the body.

Proteins are slightly different. We can't store amino acids which are the products of proteins. Therefore, we quickly lose amino acids from our system as urea if we can't use them immediately. They can also be used to complete our energy store as glycogen or fat, or for body growth and development.

Carbohydrates are important because they produce glucose for energy release. If there is insufficient glucose in our system, we call on proteins to cover this deficiency. However, as protein also plays a part in normal growth and development, there is often little left and amino acids would only be used in this way if you had not eaten for a number of days! For the swimmer, this should be avoided, for the enzymes and tissues he would be using to make the muscles work are now being depleted. This leads to a weight loss and lethargy, and he will see his personal performance regressing. The only way out of this is for him to take in more carbohydrates or reduce his training load.

For those people interested in taking up distance swimming, fat is very important as a slow burning form of energy. As I have already mentioned, fat can be found in the muscle cells. The fat is slowly used and more fat in the form of fatty acids after enzyme conversion is taken from the blood stream and converted. By comparison those people who are taking part in speed work will find that fat cannot be converted quickly enough, nor is it adequate. Carbohydrate is used here by way of the glycogen stores in the muscle fibres. Glucose from the blood stream can be called on.

So what happens in a heavy training session? Both sources are used. If the training goes on for one to two hours and more energy is continually being used, more fatty acids and glucose are used from the blood stream as the glycogen stored in the muscles will have been used up and will need replenishing.

The energy intake of a swimmer can be measured in the laboratory[8] by calculating the 24-hour energy output and weighing the food before eating and thus determine the energy intake. However body weight remains almost constant in energy balance. If this weight is constant over a period of time then energy balance is being achieved.

Energy expenditure during training depends on the weight of the person carrying it out. Energy is doubled as the speed of the swimmer doubles. Women have more body fat than men, and a subsequent increase in buoyancy along with a decrease in drag. They use about 30 per cent less energy than men swimming the same distance. Training brings greater efficiency, and after a while your energy expenditure will be reduced by some 10 per cent.

Mean Heights and Weights and Recommended Intakes

Category	Age (years)	Weight (kg)	Weight (lb)	Height (cm)	Height (in)	Energy needs (with range) (kcal)	(ml)
Males	11-14	45	99	157	62	2,700 (2,000-3,700)	11.3
	15-18	66	145	176	69	2,800 (2,100-3,900)	11.8
	19-22	70	154	177	70	2,900 (2,500-3,300)	12.2
	23-50	70	154	178	70	2,700 (2,300-3,100)	11.3
Females	11-14	46	101	157	62	2,200 (1,500-3,000)	9.2
	15-18	55	120	163	64	2,100 (1,200-3,000)	8.8
	19-22	55	120	163	64	2,100 (1,700-2,500)	8.8
	23-50	55	120	163	64	2,000 (1,600-2,400)	8.4
Diet & Supplement						3,275	

			Fat-soluble vitamins				Water-soluble vitamins					
		Pro-tein (g)	Vit A (ug RE)	Vit D (ug)	Vit E (mg a TE)	Thia-min (mg)	Vit C (mg)	Rib-ofla vin (mg)	Nia cin (mg NE)	Vit B6 (mg)	Fol-acin (ug)	Vit B12 (ug)
Males	11-14	45	1,000	10	8	1.4	50	1.6	18	1.8	300	3.0
	15-18	56	1,000	10	10	1.4	60	1.7	18	2.0	300	3.0
	19-22	56	1,000	7.5	10	1.5	60	1.7	19	2.2	300	3.0
	23-50	56	1,000	5	10	1.4	60	1.6	18	2.2	300	3.0
Females	11-14	46	800	10	8	1.1	50	1.3	15	1.8	300	3.0
	15-18	46	800	10	8	1.1	60	1.3	14	2.0	200	3.0
	19-22	44	800	7.5	8	1.1	60	1.3	14	2.0	300	3.0
	23-50	44	800	5	8	1.0	60	1.2	13	2.0	300	3.0
Diet & Supplement		135	1,400	3*	25	5.6	340	5.0	30	5.7	300	6.4

*Exposure to sunlight will compensate for the apparent deficiency of Vit D.

Minerals						
		Calcium (mg)	Phosphorus (mg)	Magnesium (mg)	Iron (mg)	Zinc (mg)
Males	11-14	1,200	1,200	350	18	15
	15-18	1,200	1,200	400	18	15
	19-22	800	800	350	10	15
	23-50	800	800	350	10	15
Females	11-14	1,200	1,200	300	18	15
	15-18	1,200	1,200	300	18	15
	19-22	800	800	300	18	15
	23-50	800	800	300	18	15
Diet & Supplement		1,800	1,700	500	33	20

Figures compiled in the USA.

Estimated Daily Calorie Requirements for Children, Adolescents and Adults

Sex and age range	Pre-training and non-training daily calorie needs		Estimated daily calorie needs in training	Training time (hours)
	Average	Per pound		
Males 10 and under	2,400	39	2,800-2,900	1
	2,700	27	3,700-4,100	2
11-14			4,700-5,500	4
15-18	2,800	19	4,800-6,000	4
19-22	2,900	19	4,900-6,100	4
23-50	2,700	18	4,700-5,500	4
Females 10 and under	2,400	39	2,800-2,900	1
	2,200	22	3,000-3,400	2
11-14			3,800-4,600	4
15-18	2,100	18	3,700-4,900	4
19-22	2,100	18	3,700-4,900	4
23-50	2,000	17	3,600-4,400	4

Calorie Expenditure for Swimming												
Activity	**Calorie needs per min., per lb. of weight**	**Calorie needs per minute at different weights**										
		50 110	**53 117**	**56 123**	**59 130**	**62 137**	**65 143**	**68 150**	**74 163**	**80 176**	**86 190**	**89 kg 196 lb**
Backstroke	0.077	8.5	9.0	9.5	10.0	10.5	11.0	11.5	12.5	13.5	14.5	15.0
Breaststroke	0.074	8.1	8.6	9.1	9.6	10.0	10.5	11.0	12.0	13.0	13.9	14.0
Crawl, fast	0.071	7.8	8.3	8.7	9.2	9.7	10.1	10.6	11.5	12.5	13.4	13.0
Crawl, slow	0.058	6.4	6.8	7.2	7.6	7.9	8.3	8.7	9.5	10.2	11.0	11.0
Side stroke	0.055	6.1	6.5	6.8	7.2	7.6	7.9	8.3	9.0	9.8	10.5	10.0
Treading, fast	0.077	8.5	9.0	9.5	10.0	10.5	11.1	11.6	12.6	13.6	14.6	15.0
Treading, normal	0.028	3.1	3.3	3.5	3.7	3.8	4.0	4.2	4.6	5.0	5.3	5.0

Adapted from W. D. McCardle, F. I. Katch, and V. L. Katch, *Exercise Physiology – Energy, Nutrition and Human Performance,* (Lea and Fabiger, Philadelphia, 1981). Reproduced in D. Wilkie and K. Juba, *Handbook of Swimming* (Pelham, 1987).

Vitamins

I haven't so far mentioned vitamins which contain minerals. They are frequently emphasized but, in general, they are needed in smaller quantities than is often claimed. Extra vitamins taken above the required amount could lead to a deterioration in performance. Calcium, iron, iodine, phosphorus and zinc are all minerals needed by the body. Vitamins don't contain energy or calories. Very broadly, iron is the only mineral deficiency which occurs regularly in Britain, particularly in women. However, deficiency in either of the water soluble vitamins (B and C) leads to a lower output of work. If, on the other hand, you take too much of B or C, it is excreted in the urine but only at an energy cost. The fat soluble vitamins (A, D, E and K) are more of a problem if taken excessively because they cannot be discharged in urine but instead remain as toxic bodies in the liver.

If you are vegetarian, this shouldn't create a problem with regard to taking the right amount of vitamins per day. A vegan needs to take B12 vitamin tablets.

Below is a table of the UK Recommended Dietary Amounts in 1979:

(ug)	Thiamin (Vit. C)	Ribloflavin (Vit. C)	Niacin (Vit. C)	Folic Acid	Ascorbic Acid	Vitamins
Males 15-17 years	1.2	1.7	19	300	30	750
Adults (active)	1.3	1.6	18	300	30	750
Females 15-17 years	0.9	1.7	19	300	30	750
Adults (active) ug = microgram	1.0	1.3	15	300	30	750

There are no recommendations for Vitamin K because bacteria manufacture it in the large intestine; Vitamin D comes to our body through the sun's rays; and Vitamin E, B6 (pyridoxine) and B12 deficiencies never arise in a healthy person on a natural diet[9].

Many studies have been carried out, but there is no evidence to suggest that vitamins can improve the performance of a swimmer. Someone who is training will find that an increased training load should be matched by an increased energy output and intake. When extra food is digested the higher vitamin requirement is included in this. You shouldn't need to pop extra pills if your diet is sufficiently varied.

For vitamin requirements based on mean weight and heights, see the table on p. 34[10]. Essolyte drinks have become a well-known way of taking vitamins, with the replacing of salt a key part. Salt loss comes about through sweating during training. These drinks can be harmful in excess and should only be taken immediately after or during the period of sweating.

The National Advisory Committee on Nutrition Education has recommended that total fat content of the diet, sucrose and alcohol should be reduced and the fibre content of the diet increased by using more cereals, fruit and vegetables.

Calories

Many of us are concerned that too high a calorie intake will increase the amount of fats in our bodies. However, food in the form of calories is essential to a swimmer's diet if he is to train. Fats and carbohydrates, which have a higher or very high calorific value, are not recommended. The table on p. 36 gives a guide to the amount of calories used whilst swimming different strokes.

Dehydration

All athletes need to maintain fluid intake to prevent dehydration. Mild dehydration can cause mild cramp, fatigue and general grogginess as well as a decrease in performance[11]. When dehydration is severe, the body will sweat in order to keep its temperature down. When this evaporation has to stop, owing to lack of fluid, the result is an uncontrolled rise of body temperature.

Swimmers can also lose body heat by conduction into the water as they swim. However, this is more difficult to achieve in warm water. If you are racing outdoors in a hot climate, it is likely that you will become dehydrated more than in an indoor competition in winter. Six to eight cups of water a day will be enough for most swimmers.

You can get a rough guide to your personal level of dehydration both when you are training or racing. Check your weight before and after training. A one pound body weight loss is equal to two cups of water. You can re-weigh afterwards and replenish on the basis of four cups of fluid per hour.

You can also use your own urine as a guide. Pale yellow urine, the colour of lemon juice is about right; dark yellow or brown means you need to increase fluid intake.

Alcohol

I mentioned earlier that alcohol intake would need to be reduced as alcohol is quickly absorbed into the blood stream. It contains an excessive amount of calories – 196 Kcals per ounce of pure alcohol. The liver has to give alcohol priority over everything else, which causes it to work overtime. The process of detoxifying alcohol accelerates the heavier you are.

To demonstrate how your swimming and general well-being could be affected, these results have been produced[12]; based on one drink of pure ethyl alcohol being equal to twelve ounces of beer, four ounces of wine or one ounce of liquor:

Amount	Blood level of alcohol	Effect
2 drinks	0.5%	Judgement impaired. Mellow feeling.
4 drinks	0.10%	Reaction time slows. Less cautious than normal. Drink too quickly, vomit reflex could be induced.
6 drinks	0.15%	Muscle co-ordination, and reflexes impaired. Reaction time slower than normal. Things begin to spin round.
8 drinks	0.20%	Vision impaired, speech and walking difficulties.

The importance of carbohydrates

The 70 per cent carbohydrate intake needs to be monitored. A rest day will allow the glycogen levels to build up in the liver and muscles. This is, therefore, important before a big event or race. Glycogen which comes from carbohydrates represents some 90 per cent of the food constituent that swimmers need for most events up to 1,500 metres.

Glucose is also an important direct form of energy for the muscle cells. Glucose tends to be used more and more as glycogen is depleted. One in five swimmers[13] will suffer adverse functioning of the brain after two hours of non-stop moderate intensity swimming. This is known as hypoglycaemia. This can be avoided by regularly eating carbohydrates when you are going to carry out long training sessions. Potatoes are an excellent source because they contain not only carbohydrates but Vitamin B complex, which is also so important to swimmers. Obviously, to eat potatoes at the optimum time of thirty minutes before a training session is not a good idea because they weigh too heavily on the stomach.

If you take solids or drinks which are high in glucose, this can trigger off the release of insulin. This, in turn, can bring on temporary hypoglycaemia. Whetton[13] recommends the ingestion of more complex carbohydrates that can take much longer to be released. These would allow carbohydrates to enter the blood stream over a period of about thirty to sixty minutes and would avoid the high release of insulin. He further recommends a liquid mixture comprising small quantities of glucose, other sugars, starches and a variety of maltodextrins or partially broken down starch molecules.

From personal experience, I feel sure that diet is equally important in long distance swimming. I can remember completing the ASA Long Distance Championship at York when 13 years of age without any clear recollection of the last two miles. This could have been hypoglycaemia. At the same age, I completed the Welsh Long Distance Championship on Lake Bala. I remember finishing but being incredibly hungry. The water was less than 53°F on both occasions and I feel sure, looking back to those days in the early 1960s, that I was inadequately prepared through ignorance of the correct diet.

A protein based drink is recommended. The reason for this is that recent studies have shown that protein is playing a more important role in the life of an active swimmer than was previously thought. Until recently, it was considered that a swimmer needed no more protein than an average person. Without it, the muscle fibres appear to be more damaged than was originally realized, and the muscles stiffen after exercise. This occurs on the first day after exercise and heightens on the second, and can even damage these muscles. Protein should therefore be taken to help overcome this at a suggested rate of 1.2 to 1.5 grams per kilogram of body weight.

Eating before competition

Any competition or event produces nervous tension, and tension causes a decrease of blood flow to your stomach and small intestine. This, in turn, slows down the chemical reactions needed to produce energy for the event ahead. Food already in your intestine and stomach will stay there until the blood supply returns to normal. Nerves can manifest themselves in other ways. Stress increases acid in your stomach, making it feel tight – as though it has butterflies. Your lower intestine is affected and brings about an increased likelihood of diarrhoea.

The effects of pre-event eating can be as much mental as physical. Different people react differently to the same foods, and some feel that eating certain foods will help them win. Bear in mind three factors:

1 Your stomach should be empty when you compete. Foods which are fatty and take a long while to digest are to be avoided.
2 You should have sufficient water in your body to avoid dehydration.
3 The energy or calories taken before the event should be sufficient for you both to compete at your best and to prevent your feeling weak or hungry.

A small meal between two and four hours before you compete will benefit you most. About 300–500 calories is all you need, and the meal should be comprised of complex carbohydrates that will take time to break down. Cyclam, glucose, dextrose and simple carbohydrates should be avoided at this stage, as the sugar from these will enter the blood stream for a short period of time only and lead to an eventual drop in sugar level. You may feel weak and tired.

If you take a food which combines complex carbohydrates with a little protein and fat, the protein and fat will help to prevent the sugar level in your blood moving too high or too low. If the food contains too much protein prior to competition, it will encourage the body to do jobs other than to prepare its muscles for competition. There are various liquid meals of this nature on the market.

The timing of your water intake is also important. Ideally you should drink one cup of water for every fifty pounds you weigh about two hours before competition, and one or two cups fifteen minutes beforehand. Coffee, tea and any drinks which contain caffeine should be avoided at this stage because caffeine lifts the heart rate and increases nervousness.

Here are some pre-competition foods:

Pre-Competition Meal Ideas		
Sports Food-Swap Group	**Food choice**	**Average calories**
Grain	1½ cup cereal	150
Dairy	with 1 cup low-fat milk	125
Fruit	Banana	80
Grain	1 slice of whole grain toast	70
Sweets	with 1 teaspoon jam	20
		445
Grain	Turkey sandwich	
	2 slices whole grain bread	140
High protein Meat	2 ounces turkey	150
Vegetable	1 sliced tomato	25
Fat	1 tsp. salad dressing	45
Fruit	1 apple	80
		440
Grain	1 cup pasta	140
Vegetable	with 1 cup tomato-mushroom sauce	50
Fat	(1 tsp. oil in sauce)	45
Vegetable	1 cup salad – lettuce, tomatoes with	
	lemon juice	50
Fruit	1 pear	40
Dairy	1 cup low-fat milk	125
		450

Swimming World, January 1985

Some winners aim to get down to what they regard as their best weight for a race. Avoid doing this. Keep your weight constant before competition. Any weight loss of more than one or two pounds a week will decrease endurance and aerobic capacity.

Eating during the event

Fluid levels need to be maintained in the body. You need to get your fluid level up before the meet by following the drinking plan suggested. Drinking just to satisfy your thirst during a competition is not enough. You need to drink one or two cups of fluid every half-hour. Take small amounts of fluids on a regular basis, particularly if you are in a day's competition which involves a lot of waiting around. If you are going to compete several times, you want to avoid your stomach feeling full and bloated with water, and your stomach can only absorb about one pint of fluid an hour.

Energy levels also have to be maintained. This means maintaining your glycogen stores and your blood sugar level at a steady level. This can be done by scheduling in small meals as long as there is a reasonable time to digest them. Eating small amounts of carbohydrates before and during events will leave your stomach empty during the competition, which is helpful as the stomach doesn't feel too heavy.

Those who are entering long distance swimming competitions will need to replace both energy and water losses in a fluid which is easy to drink. Best of all are the fruit and vegetable juices which have been diluted so that the sugar concentration is isotonic, i.e. the same as your body fluid. This will help to keep your blood sugar in balance.

After the competition both your fluid level and energy concentration will need to return to their normal level. This can happen naturally, but many swimmers don't feel like eating immediately after competition. Your first concern will probably be to drink and replace fluid, and this tends to be easier to do at this stage.

Carbohydrate loading
This has been used by many athletes in recent years to improve performance through diet by controlling carbohydrate intake. It requires control for seven days before the competition.

For the first three days the swimmer eats a low carbohydrate diet, aiming to keep fats and protein steady. On the first day a two-hour session of the toughest nature should be carried out to deplete the muscles of glycogen. Because the swimmer's diet is based on low carbohydrate, it prevents adequate replacement over the next two days. As a result, the enzymes normally responsible for glycogen conversion are more active than normal.

On the fourth day, the swimmer changes to a high carbohydrate diet with 70-80 per cent of calories being carbohydrate. This is maintained for three days. Because of the extra active enzymes and availability of carbohydrates, your muscles will have at their disposal two or three times the normal amount of glycogen. This would all be coupled with relatively easy training programmes so that this level of glycogen isn't reduced before competition begins.

The swimmer has to determine whether or not the extra weight he will carry will be a disadvantage. In addition, one wonders whether this type of diet control may be more relevant to sportsmen and women other than swimmers, with the possible exception of those people who want to race over 1,500 metres or are in long distance training. In most shorter events, the body would have a sufficiently high level of glycogen quite naturally. Professor Clyde Williams at Loughborough University feels that the same effect can be achieved with a good taper and a very high carbohydrate diet.

A Guide to Where to Find Ingredients			
Carbohydrates		**Proteins**	**Unsaturated and polyunsaturated fats**
Potatoes (steamed or baked)	Scones	Milk	Margarine
	Pancakes	Cheese	Low generic forms of butter
Carrots	Teacakes	Corn (maize)	Olive oil
Peas	Biscuits	Eggs	Nuts
Corn	Cake	Meat (muscle)	Cooking oil
Apple	Pasta	Peas	Skimmed milk
Grapefruit	Spaghetti	Wheat	
Plums	Macaroni	Gelatin	
Pears	Tapioca	Fish	**Saturated fats**
Raisins	Rice	Dried beans	Cake
Dates	Sago		Cheese
Apricots	Jam		Butter
Figs	Sugar		Chips
Bread	Sweets		Food cooked in fat
Rolls	Honey		Milk
French loaf	Chocolate		

8 JOINING A CLUB

In Chapter 1, I emphasized the need to determine one's objectives. In order to help you decide, here are some of the activities possible:

Subject	Age	Aim	Opportunities
Race – sprint swimming	16-21	To win championships	Local club or training scheme
	22-80	Masters championships	Local club or Masters club
Fun swimming – all distances	16-21	Fitness	Local club
	22-90	Fitness	Adult lane at pool
Race – middle and long distance swimming	16-21	To win championships	Local club or training scheme
	22-80	Masters championships	Local club or Masters club
Long distance swimming – open water	16-80	To win long distance events/fun/swim the Channel	Local BLDSA club
Disabled swimming	16-80	To keep fit/compete against others on equal basis	Local disabled group

The opportunities swimming provides are endless. It provides the basis, through safety and confidence in water, for anyone who wants to take up other water sports – board sailing, canoeing, sailing, waterskiing, surfing and sub aqua diving. There are also various branches of swimming itself. Men can take part in diving, life saving or water polo to a relatively old age; women can join them in diving and life saving, and have further opportunities with synchronized swimming. With the exception of diving, you have to be fit and able to swim well before you can carry out the other activities.

Naturally there are many adults who just want to swim to be fit. Advanced adult groups are now organized by local councils, and the ASA have an adult award scheme to provide incentives. The Swim Fit Awards are solely for distance swimming, and have no requirements for speed or style. The swimmer has a record card and the awards are as follows:

10 miles – yellow	200 miles – sage green
20 miles – mid blue	250 miles – red
40 miles – orange	300 miles – turquoise
60 miles – dark green	350 miles – silver
80 miles – fawn	400 miles – slate grey
100 miles – clover	450 miles – mid green
150 miles – dark blue	500 miles – pink

For those who wish to race, many swimming clubs now accept older swimmers for training. The best opportunities for adults are normally to be found with the less high-powered competitive clubs who are not looking to produce top-flight young swimmers.

In 1969, Masters swimming was introduced into Britain. This form of competition gave adult swimmers the chance to compete in five-year age-group bands in the same way as young age-group swimmers have competed for years. The following Masters events are programmed at our National Masters Championships:

Masters Championships (Events for both men and women)											
Age:	25-29	30-34	35-39	40-44	45-49	50-54	55-59	60-64	65-69	70-74	75-99
Free 50	•	•	•	•	•	•	•	•	•	•	•
Free 100	•	•	•	•	•	•	•				
Free 200	•	•	•	•	•	•	•	•	•	•	•
Back 50	•	•	•	•	•	•	•	•	•	•	W only
Back 100	•	•	•	•	•	•	•				
Breast 50	•	•	•	•	•	•	•	•	•	•	•
Breast 100	•	•	•	•	•	•	•				
Fly 50	•	•	•	•	•	•	•	•	•	•	M only
Fly 100	•	•	•	•	•	•	•				
Individual Medley 100	•	•	•	•	•	•	•	•	•	•	•

Masters clubs now exist in their own right for adult women and men who wish to train together, enjoy one another's company and compete in competitions together.

Long distance swimming now has its own organization, although the British LDSA is affiliated to the ASA. There are both professional and amateur competitions; in Britain, however, all events are amateur. Some of the regular annual events on the national calendar are:

Place	Distance (miles)	Place	Distance (miles)
Windermere (two-way)	21	Coniston	5¼
Bala (two-way)	6	Cross Tay (double)	1¾
Pickmere	3	Torbay	7½ (Veterans 3¾)
Exmouth Fairway	4½	ASA Holmepierrepont	5
Southsea Pier to Pier	3	Derwentwater Triangle	5

Squad sessions which are not overcrowded can help, as can the discipline of regularly working in a group. Here we see a lane of swimmers who have been given five second gaps before each start and are using the 'chain' system.

For those ambitious to go further, European and World Masters Championships are held on a cyclical basis, both open to anyone.

The cost of joining a swimming coaching scheme where a professional coach works for a local authority is normally around £13–15 per month, plus entry to the pool, if you are going to train regularly. The major problem here is that such schemes are normally geared to people who are between 12 and 18 and still at school. The clubs therefore tend to train at unsuitable times for adults who are working. It is much better to join a Masters club, but these are few and far between.

One alternative is to form an ad hoc group with two or three friends; another is to join one of the fitness schemes for adults which many councils are now introducing. The cost of these is generally about £7–8.

Remember, if you want to compete in races in Britain, you have to be a member of a club affiliated to one of the member associations of the Great Britain Swimming Federation (see appendix).

9 TRAINING METHODS AND PROGRAMMES

The type of training programme you use will depend on your own experience as much as anything else. Most methods and programmes are specially developed by individuals for themselves. Yours has to produce the best performance from you. Variety has an important part to play. It is easy to get bored in training, with your head in the water most of the time and hardly anyone with whom to communicate. Variety should mean changes of strokes and distances at regular intervals.

Each training session, however, should include a solid bank of work, either swum as a straight distance or broken up into repetitions. The purpose behind this is to provide regular training on the rhythm of your stroke and to rehearse the movement continually. This solid bank needs to be swum on a fast stroke in order to get through as much work as possible in the allocated time available. Speed can be developed through this endurance base, but endurance cannot come through a programme of short sprints.

Assuming you are now reasonably fit, what then are some of the more important types of training? The best known are as follows:

Fartlek – or speed play This is little used now but is useful whilst getting even fitter. It consists of changing speed and distance on a slightly haphazard basis in order to build up general feel on a distance swim.

Locomotive swimming Here fast swimming alternates with slow, and the distances gradually go up. The swimmer starts with one fast length, one slow length, two fast, two slow, and so on up to, for instance, six lengths of each before going back to one. In a 25 metre pool, this will mean that the swimmer has covered 1,800 metres. Further varieties can be introduced, perhaps by swimming each cycle (ones, twos, threes, etc) in individual medley order or else by alternating two strokes throughout.

Repetition swimming Here a swimmer completes a series of swims, each broken up into a regular series of short distances. The repetitions are swum at a medium pace.

Controlled interval swimming This has been the basic method used by most competitive swimmers since its introduction from athletics in the 1960s. It consists of a series of repetitions of a similar distance with a constant length of time for each swim and rest. For example, you might complete 10 × 100 metres on your second stroke, starting each 100 metre swim every two minutes (i.e. 2 minutes = swim + rest). As you get more pace control, you will learn what sort of times you ought to be achieving. For instance, if you know that you can swim each 100 metres in 70 seconds, you can regard each repetition as a speed swim; if it is taking 1 minute 45 seconds, it becomes an endurance-based swim.

Descending series This follows the pattern of the CIM swim (i.e. with constant leaving time) but the swimmer aims to get faster with each swim until the last repetition is in his fastest time or close to it.

Regressive series Like the descending series, these are essentially to build up pace. They consist of a series of swims which go from fastest to slowest. These are probably psychologically not as good as either CIM or the descending series.

Broken swims These tend to be used more when swimmers are tapering before events. They help to bring the swimmer psychologically to a peak. The swimmer might still swim his 10 × 100 metres but he would increase the pace and improve the times by taking a five or ten second break after each 25 or 50 metres.

Alternating swims Here the swimmer alternates one set with another set. This is mostly for variety, and might consist of 6 × 200 metres freestyle alternating with 6 × 100 metres backstroke – with a 30-second rest after each swim.

Mixed swims These again are primarily for variety. The swimmer mixes two sets of different strokes of an entirely different nature. He might be swimming 6 × 400 metres freestyle off 5 minutes 30 seconds. This might be spliced with 4 × 50 metres butterfly every 1 minute after the second and fourth freestyle swims.

High quality or goal training

Attempts have been made recently to invent a new kind of training method, the aim being to design a way of measuring the intensity of each training session so that training can be tailored to the needs of each individual. Work has been carried out by Dr J. Counsilman of Indiana University[14,15], who identified two possible types of series which he called 'goal sets' and 'cruise sets'. Counsilman related that his swimmers could just about achieve 1,000 metres in goal sets. These are high speed sets with a long rest, targeting for specific times; but when swimmers do them with maximum effort they take a number of days to recover.

Counsilman believes that Masters swimmers need to build up to this steadily by doing shorter sets until able to cope with what was at one time known as a High Quality Set. In all the above types of swimming the swimmer is training aerobically (with air). The whole feel is quite different.

Continuous use of high quality swimming would push the swimmer into a situation where his body no longer adapts. These methods should be used sparingly in the four week taper period before a major race (see Chapter 11), and even then only as short sets, varying the distances involved.

Cruise training

Cruise sets, a term first used by American coach Dick Bower, are the opposite to High Quality. This type of training concentrates on the cardio-vascular system and incorporates short rests. Bower has termed the cruise interval as equalling the fastest departure interval at which an individual can swim 5 × 100 metres repeat swims, plus five seconds. The cruise interval time for other distances can be determined by doubling the cruise time for the 200, quadrupling it for the 400 and so on, so that it is always in proportion to the interval.

Counsilman[16] provided the following chart to determine this:

Cruise Interval Target Table								⊙
swims	50m	75m	100m	150m	200m	300m	400m	500m
Time in minutes and seconds								
Senior men	30.0/ 35.0	45.0/ 52.0	1.00/ 1.10	1.30/ 1.45	2.00/ 2.20	3.00/ 3.30	4.00/ 4.40	5.00/ 5.50
Senior women	32.5/ 37.5	42.5/ 55.0	1.05/ 1.15	1.32/ 1.50	2.10/ 2.30	3.15/ 3.45	4.20/ 5.00	5.25/ 6.15
Age groups 12-14 Masters 25-34	35.0/ 40.0	47.5/ 60.0	1.10/ 1.20	1.45/ 2.00	2.20/ 2.40	3.30/ 4.00	4.40/ 5.20	5.50 6.40
Age groups 11-12 Masters 34-49	37.5/ 42.5	50.0/ 1.05	1.15/ 1.25	1.52/ 2.07	2.30/ 2.50	3.45/ 4.15	5.00/ 5.40	6.15/ 7.05
Age groups 9-10 Masters 50-59	40.0/ 45.0	52.5/ 1.10	1.20/ 1.30	2.00/ 2.20	2.40/ 3.00	4.00/ 4.30	5.20/ 6.00	6.40/ 7.30
Masters 60+ Competitive beginners 8-12	42.5/ 47.5	55.0/ 1.12.5	1.25/ 1.35	2.07.5/ 2.25	2.50/ 3.10	4.15/ 4.45	5.40/ 6.20	7.05/ 7.55

The heart rate should be at about 150 to 180 beats a minute, with the swimmer resting for 5–10 seconds between repetitions. As each month goes by your short rest or, as it is now known, cruise interval should drop. Your average time for each series of repetitions should also go down.

The cruise interval is determined by taking the average time of 5 × 100 metres originally used, multiplying it by the increase in distance and adding the following increments[17]:

	100	200	300	400	500	800
	1 × AT*	2 × AT	3 × AT	4 × AT	5 × AT	8 × AT
Seconds added	2-4	5-11	9-18	13-25	18-32	35-48

*Average time of original 5 × 100 metres. The slower the swimmer, the greater the time increments.

Bower recommends that the cruise speed should be tested[18] on a swim of 6×100 metres, normally in the middle or at the end of a training session.

Hypoxic training

Hypoxic training concentrates mainly on overloading the lungs. Swimmers are asked to swim freestyle or butterfly for a certain number of strokes before taking a breath. Not only does it build up breath control for sprint races and teach the swimmer to take fewer breaths in a sprint; it creates an overload situation and enables the swimmer to keep his head down at the end of a race.

You might, for instance, train for 6×200 metres. On the first repetition, you might breathe every stroke; on the second, every two strokes; on the third, every three strokes, and so on. You might want to carry out this breathing pattern on each length instead of each repetition. Hypoxic training began as a way of carrying out endurance training and obtaining a similar effect.

Construction training sessions

This, again, is very personal. There are certain factors that you can monitor even if you are training on your own. You should aim to balance the aerobic and anaerobic parts of the session. This means exercising discipline in your swimming sessions; with three things to aim at:

1 Regular stroke counting so that you keep the strokes per length constant.
2 Every time you return to a series of repetitions that you have logged before, the repetitions should show a progressive improvement in times.
3 Your pulse count, which may be on about 180 beats per minute when you start your anaerobic work, should drop steadily throughout your training year.

Try to put your training sessions together in such a way that your rests are short. Your speed early in the season will be about 70–80 per cent of race speed. Later in the year, this will improve to 75–85 per cent. Your anaerobic threshold will limit this.

In the course of each week you will need to try to mix the three main areas: sprint training (often seen as power); anaerobic training (where the body is trying to learn to live with its lactic acid build-up and to train to handle more); and aerobic training (where your body is trying to handle work with sufficient oxygen brought to its system). Your main set should last for no less than twenty minutes to be beneficial – preferably thirty minutes. Get to know your maximum heart rate in terms of beats per minute. If you are training on your own you can test it regularly. You might decide, for instance, to try to swim a set of repetitions to build up your aerobic capacity. If you are fit, your pulse will be around 210 beats per minute. Astrand (1965) stated that the maximum heart rate achievable should be 210 beats − age × 0.65. You need to know what it should be before you start such a set. The set would probably comprise something like $20 \times 50m + 3$ min. or $12 \times 100m + 4$ min.

A set of work which allows us to recover from a very hard series before going on to another main block of work is called a recovery set. It generally consists of a set of kicking swims or a long swim at about 60 per cent effort.

The construction of a training session should therefore look something like this:

Set	Example distance	Reason
Warm-up	600m – arms, legs, stroke lengths in order	Loosen up – develop feel for water
Sprints	$8 \times 50 + 2$ min. 3rd choice	Work on speed early whilst still fresh and whilst your muscles still have high pH
Main set	8×200 off 2½ min. 1st choice	Aerobic body of endurance-based work
Kick	8×75 kick + 10 sec. 2nd choice	Overload of muscles in legs
Sprints	$10 \times 25 + 1½$ min. 1st choice	Working on lactate build-up

Other training aids

There are other aids that you might like to introduce into your training session.

Surgical tubing attached to the end of the pool and then to the swimmer can help to develop strength. Most coaches do this over fairly short swims of up to thirty seconds.

There are also hand paddles, with which you can work on better hand positioning. If you have pain in one shoulder, then you can rest that arm by using a hand paddle while the other arm pulls and does the work. It's a good way of concentrating on the pull position on one arm.

You may also want to use flippers. These overload the feet and legs and put the accent on ankle flexibility. Some people even kick with plimsolls. This works the muscles of the lower leg extremely hard. Similarly, the use of a drag suit or swimming in a tee-shirt is a good way of overloading the arms and upper body.

Training on your own

Many readers will be intending, or may be obliged, to train on their own throughout most of the year. A good clock with a second hand at the pool will, therefore, be important to you. You should be well acquainted with it in relation to your own pace, day in, day out.

You can make the timing simpler by always setting off when the hands of the clock are at the top or the bottom of the clock, or at some easily memorable position. Alternatively it might be possible to purchase a waterproof digital sportswatch that has a reversible count-down or count-up mode. Here, all you need to do is to set the interval, and the watch tells you when to start your next swim. With the count-up, you can also get the watch to tell you what your time is for the repeat.

If you are not fortunate enough to own a waterproof digital watch, a descending or reducing series of swims will help you to get used to using the clock. You should make a point of doing this early on, until you get to know your pace.

Types of training

Each area of training has a different quality. You need to be aware of these in designing your programme. They are as follows:

Type	Physiological area	Purpose
Long (or over) race distance swims, e.g. 2 × 1,500 or 3 × 800 + 15 sec.	Aerobic	Cardio-vascular and local muscular endurance
Kicking or pulling segments, e.g. 10 × 100 + 15 sec.	Aerobic	Local muscular endurance
Cruise interval swims, e.g. 20 × 150 + 10 sec.	Aerobic	This is nearly all cardio-vascular endurance: there is a little aerobic work here
Lactate work, e.g. 6 × 100 + 5 min.	Anaerobic	Develops ability to keep a relatively high speed for as long as possible in a race. This period is not normally long and will be increased through this
Sprints 30 × 50 off 1 min.	Anaerobic	Works on explosive sprint power and speed

Stroke drills

Stroke drills provide variety and are beneficial during the winter months in that they enable the swimmer to work on any technical faults which need to be overcome. Essentially drills allow the swimmer to divide the stroke into parts in order to isolate one limb or part of a movement and to concentrate on it. There is a danger of working on too many drills to the detriment of swimming complete strokes. I would recommend that not more than ten per cent of your training session should be spent on drills. There are literally hundreds of different drills that you could use. Here are some of them:

Purpose	Drill
Front crawl 1. Single arm – other arm on surface of water, stretched out on centre line	Correct positioning of hand during pull
2. Catch up freestyle – both arms recover normally but one arm pauses on being stretched out in front, the other catches it up	Good position to ensure the correct catch of the water
3. Front crawl with head out of water	You can watch hand position on entry and pull. Overloads the leg kick. Concentrate on centring up hands
4. Bilateral freestyle – the sequence is to breathe to one side, take three strokes and breathe to the other side	As above

5. Hand flick at end of pull – the hands are pushing past the hips and overemphasised in pushing up towards roof	Final part of pull. Ensures completion of pull past hips
6. Monkey swimming – normal swimming, but everytime arm is recovered, fingers touch underside of armpit before entering water	Gets swimmer used to high elbow recovery
7. Finger scrape – again normal swimming, but fingers scrape surface as hands recover forward over water	Concentrates on good hand position with fingers low during recovery

Backstroke

1. Single arm backstroke – same pattern as in freestyle	Works on correct hand entry position
2. Single arm with shoulder lift	The swimmer can work on shoulder roll with deeper hand position
3. Double arm entry backstroke – instead of entering one arm at time, both arms enter together	Good for ensuring correct hand position throughout pull
4. Final phase – double arms. Swimmer merely pulls both arms underwater until level with shoulders; he then pushes back to hips	Concentrates on pushing back at end of pull
5. Right arm, left arm, both arms backstroke – this swum with normal kick	Swimmer can work on correct hand entry

Butterfly

1. Dive butterfly – swimmer dives head and upper body half a metre into water on entering arms	Assists kick – swimmer trains with hips completely surrounded by water
2. Single arm butterfly – opposite arm straight out in front in water. Swimmer breathes to side	Concentration of right hand entry
3. Butterfly with head out	Increases resistance on legs
4. Butterfly kick on one side with one arm on water, head resting on it, other arm by side	As in 1
5. Butterfly swum on back or butterfly without arm action on back	Mainly for variety – swimmer can actually see position of legs
6. Kick with one leg, other leg remains static. Can be done with or without float	Gets correct leg action on one leg
7. Butterfly with hands aiming to touch together in front of face before entering or on entering	Builds shoulder flexibility
8. Dolphin kick with hands clasped together behind back – bounce stomach up and down	Swimmer gets used to using hips and upper legs

Breaststroke

1. Breaststroke kick with hands in front – egg beater kick – one leg first followed by the other	Builds local endurance in legs
2. Leg kick with four large floats	Overloads ankles. Strengthens leg kick
3. One hand behind back – full stroke breaststroke – other arm pulls. Swimmer lifts heels to touch other arm	Strengthens leg action
4. Stroke swum with a sculling like pull – gets bigger during drill	Swimmer gets used to using forearms and wrist in pull
5. Leg action on back or prone with hands by sides and heels lifted to touch hands	Again, this overloads legs
6. One breaststroke pull followed by three kicks	Swimmer works on getting heels up to behind
7. Single arm breaststroke – one arm pulls, then the other, followed by both together	The swimmer can work on correct hand and wrist position
8. Three strokes with a dolphin kick followed by three strokes with a breaststroke kick	It's possible to work on shoulder and hip rotation as they follow hands in recovery

Planning your season

The whole of your training programme will lack purpose unless it is geared to a specific target. For the majority of people there will be a peak at a swimming competition; this may even become an annual target. There could be alternative targets such as the completion of a long distance swim or of a programme of yardage in which a swimmer has been aiming for a certain distance. Nevertheless, an eventual simple target performance will remain part of the strategy.

The right way to approach your season is to start at your target and work back, building your whole season around the target.

In order to be able to cope with these factors, the swimmer will need to log everything he does, so that he is constantly able to evaluate what he is doing. At the beginning of each week he should know his meterage target for the week, the number of sessions planned, and the main aim behind the week's training programme. I'm assuming that most adult swimmers will have to produce their own programme and log their own results. There would be little technical support in coaching terms. Land conditioning should be an integral part of your overall programme.

In Britain, we have run what we call a two season year for a number of years. It was introduced from America as an extension of their college and university programme and consists of a short course (25 metres or less) season, culminating in the Short Course National Championships at the start of April, and the Long Course Championships (50 metres/55 yards) held in August.

Last year the short course event was held in December, and this format will be continued. For the purposes of senior swimmers, I have assumed that a Masters swimmer will want to reach a minor peak in May, when his regional championships or an invitation competition is being held, and the major peak in July at, for instance, the Masters Nationals. If you are slightly younger and entering the Short Course Nationals in your country, then the whole programme will need to be altered to cater for an important peak in December.

Many swimmers of sixty and over have more time in which to train than those between forty and sixty. I have therefore borne this in mind in the following table assuming swimming training season starts in August:

Suggested Target Distance – Week by week					
For average fitness swimmer: target distance/number of sessions per week/length of sessions in hours					
Age 16-35	25-30	30-40	40-50	50-60	60+
Aug. 20,000	20,000	20,000	16,000	16,000	16,000
week 1 5,000/2/2	5,000/2/2	5,000/2/2	4,000/2/2	4,000/2/2	4,000/2/2
2 5,000/2/2	5,000/2/2	5,000/2/2	4,000/2/2	4,000/2/2	4,000/2/2
3 5,000/2/2	5,000/2/2	5,000/2/2	4,000/2/2	4,000/2/2	4,000/2/2
4 5,000/2/2	5,000/2/2	5,000/2/2	4,000/2/2	4,000/2/2	4,000/2/2
Sep. 32,000	28,000	28,000	20,000	20,000	20,000
week 1 8,000/3/3	7,000/3/3	7,000/3/3	5,000/3/3	5,000/3/3	5,000/3/3
2 8,000/3/3	7,000/3/3	7,000/3/3	5,000/3/3	5,000/3/3	5,000/3/3
3 8,000/3/3	7,000/3/3	7,000/3/3	5,000/3/3	5,000/3/3	5,000/3/3
4 8,000/3/3	7,000/3/3	7,000/3/3	5,000/3/3	5,000/3/3	5,000/3/3
Oct. 36,000	32,000	32,000	24,000	24,000	24,000
week 1 9,000/3/3	8,000/3/3	8,000/3/3	6,000/3/2½	6,000/3/2½	6,000/3/2½
2 9,000/3/3	8,000/3/3	8,000/3/3	6,000/3/2½	6,000/3/2½	6,000/3/2½
3 9,000/3/3	8,000/3/3	8,000/3/3	6,000/3/2½	6,000/3/2½	6,000/3/2½
4 9,000/3/3	8,000/3/3	8,000/3/3	6,000/3/2½	6,000/3/2½	6,000/3/2½
Nov. 48,000	48,000	36,000	24,000	24,000	24,000
week 1 12,000/4/4	12,000/4/5	9,000/3/4	6,000/3/3	6,000/3/3	6,000/3/3
2 12,000/4/4	12,000/4/5	9,000/3/4	6,000/3/3	6,000/3/3	6,000/3/3

Age	16-35	25-30	30-40	40-50	50-60	60+
3	12,000/4/4	12,000/4/5	9,000/3/4	6,000/3/3	6,000/3/3	6,000/3/3
4	12,000/4/4	12,000/4/5	9,000/3/4	6,000/3/3	6,000/3/3	6,000/3/3
Dec.	52,000	52,000	40,000	32,000	28,000	28,000
week 1	13,000/4/4	13,000/4/4	10,000/4/4	8,000/4/4	7,000/4/4	7,000/4/4
2	13,000/4/4	13,000/4/4	10,000/4/4	8,000/4/4	7,000/4/4	7,000/4/4
3	13,000/4/4	13,000/4/4	10,000/4/4	8,000/4/4	7,000/4/4	7,000/4/4
4	13,000/4/4	13,000/4/4	10,000/4/4	8,000/4/4	7,000/4/4	7,000/4/4
Jan.	56,000	52,000	44,000	36,000	32,000	32,000
week 1	14,000/4/4	13,000/4/4	11,000/4/4½	9,000/4/4½	8,000/4/4	8,000/4/4
2	14,000/4/4	13,000/4/4	11,000/4/4½	9,000/4/4½	8,000/4/4	8,000/4/4
3	14,000/4/4	13,000/4/4	11,000/4/4½	9,000/4/4½	8,000/4/4	8,000/4/4
4	14,000/4/4	13,000/4/4	11,000/4/4½	9,000/4/4½	8,000/4/4	8,000/4/4
Feb.	60,000	60,000	50,000	40,000	40,000	40,000
week 1	15,000/5/5	15,000/5/5½	12,500/5/5	10,000/5/5	10,000/5/5	10,000/5/5
2	15,000/5/5	15,000/5/5½	12,500/5/5	10,000/5/5	10,000/5/5	10,000/5/5
3	15,000/5/5	15,000/5/5½	12,500/5/5	10,000/5/5	10,000/5/5	10,000/5/5
4	15,000/5/5	15,000/5/5½	12,500/5/5	10,000/5/5	10,000/5/5	10,000/5/5
Mar.	70,000	64,000	52,000	44,000	44,000	44,000
week 1	17,500/5/5	16,000/5/5	13,000/5/5	11,000/5/5	11,000/5/5	11,000/5/5
2	17,500/5/5	16,000/5/5	13,000/5/5	11,000/5/5	11,000/5/5	11,000/5/5
3	17,500/5/5	16,000/5/5	13,000/5/5	11,000/5/5	11,000/5/5	11,000/5/5
4	17,500/5/5	16,000/5/5	13,000/5/5	11,000/5/5	11,000/5/5	11,000/5/5

Age	16-35	25-30	30-40	40-50	50-60	60+
Apr.	39,000	39,000	35,000	33,000	32,000	32,000
week 1	12,000/5/5½	12,000/5/5	11,000/5/5	10,000/5/5	11,000/4/4	11,000/4/4
2	10,000/5/5	10,000/5/5	10,000/5/5	9,000/5/5	9,000/4/4	9,000/4/4
3	9,000/5/5	9,000/5/5	8,000/5/5	9,000/5/5	7,000/4/4	7,000/4/4
Event 4	8,000/5/5	8,000/5/5	6,000/5/5	5,000/5/5	5,000/4/4	5,000/4/4
May	58,500/	58,500/	48,000	42,000	42,000	42,000
week 1	12,000/5/5	12,000/5/5	11,000/5/5	10,000/5/5	10,000/5/5	10,000/5/5
2	14,000/5/5	14,000/5/5	12,000/5/5	10,000/5/5	10,000/5/5	10,000/5/5
3	15,000/5/5	15,000/5/5	12,500/5/5	11,000/5/5	11,000/5/5	11,000/5/5
4	17,500/5/5	17,500/5/5	12,500/5/5	11,000/5/5	11,000/5/5	11,000/5/5
Jun.	72,000	68,500	54,500	47,500	47,500	47,500
week 1	18,000/5/5	17,000/5/5	13,000/5/5	11,500/5/5	11,500/5/5	11,500/5/5
2	18,000/5/5	17,000/5/5	13,500/5/5	12,000/5/5	12,000/5/5	12,000/5/5
3	18,000/5/5	17,000/5/5	14,000/5/5	12,000/5/5	12,000/5/5	12,000/5/5
4	18,000/5/5	17,500/5/5	14,000/5/5	12,000/5/5	12,000/5/5	12,000/5/5
Jul.	39,000	38,000	30,000	26,500	25,500	25,500
week 1	19,000/5/5	19,000/5/5	15,000/5/5	13,000/5/5	12,500/5/5	12,500/5/5
Event 2	20,000/5/5	19,000/5/5	15,000/5/5	13,500/5/5	13,000/5/5	13,000/5/5
3	Easy swimming					
4	Rest					

Suggested Land Conditioning Programme Monthly

Key: Discipline × no. of sessions × time (hours) F = flexibility W = weights & strengthening work E = endurance work (running, circuit training)

Age	16-25	25-30	30-40	40-50	50-60	60+
Sep.	F×2×½	F×2×½	F×1×½	F×1×½	F×1×½	F×1×½
	W×1×½	W×1×½	W×1×½	W×1×½	W×1×½	W×1×½
	E×1×½	E×1×½	E×1×½			
Oct.	F×2×½	F×2×½	F×1×½	F×1×½	F×1×½	F×1×½
	W×1×½	W×1×½	W×1×½	W×1×½	W×1×½	W×1×½
	E×1×½	E×1×½	E×1×½			
Nov.	F×2×½	F×2×½	F×2×½	F×2×½	F×2×½	F×2×½
	W×2×½	W×2×½	W×2×½	W×1×½		
Dec.	F×3×½	F×3×½	F×3×½	F×3×½	F×3×½	F×3×½
	W×2×1	W×2×1	W×2×½	W×2×½		
Jan.	F×4×½	F×4×½	F×4×½	F×4×½	F×4×½	F×4×½
	W×2×1	W×2×1	W×2×1	W×2×¾		
Feb.	F×4×½	F×4×½	F×4×½	F×4×½	F×4×½	F×4×½
	W×2×1	W×2×1	W×2×1	W×2×¾		
Mar.	F×5×½	F×5×½	F×4×½	F×4×½	F×4×½	F×4×½
	W×2×1	W×2×1	W×2×1	W×2×¾		
Apr.	F×5×½	F×5×½	F×4×½	F×4×½	F×4×½	F×4×½
	W×1×½	W×1×½	W×1×½	W×1×½		
May	F×5×¾	F×5×¾	F×5×½	F×5×½	F×5×½	F×5×½
	W×2×1	W×2×1	W×2×¾	W×1×¾		
Jun.	F×5×1	F×5×1	F×5×¾	F×5×¾	F×5×1	F×5×1
	W×2×1	W×2×1	W×2×¾	W×2×¾		
Jul.	F×5×1	F×5×1	F×5×¾	F×5×¾	F×5×1	F×5×1
	W×2×1	W×2×1	W×2×¾	W×2×¾		
Aug.	F×5×1	F×5×1	F×5×¾	F×5×¾	F×5×¾	F×5×¾
	W×2×½	W×2×½	W×2×½	W×2×½		

Phases of the Swimming Season
All Age Groups

September – December: Preparation phase

1 Work on stroke technique – level of improvement depends on whether coaching support is available.

2 Build up endurance base through aerobic work. Develop range of strokes.

3 Work on early endurance prior to transfer to endurance attainment in water.

4 Go on to work on strength and flexibility, i.e. qualities difficult to obtain in water.

January – April: Pre-competitive phase

1 Work on aerobic threshold and VO2 maximum in water.

2 Keep up aerobic/endurance base of water work.

3 Increase strength and flexibility levels on land.

4 Go for race pace timing – adapt the body to anaerobic repeats.

5 Develop pace instinct.

6 Introduce starts and turns training.

7 Overload all systems to a greater extent in water.

May – August: Competitive phase

1 Work on all three race phases – aerobic/anaerobic/sprint.

2 Sharpen up on starts and turns.

3 Maintain flexibility but drop power work slightly.

4 Increase speed loading – do not over-sprint.

5 Refine technique.

6 Develop race or event strategy – mental approach to training.

64

10 GETTING STRONGER

Land conditioning needs to include a general mix of endurance, strength and particularly flexibility training. It needs to supplement your water training and not replace it. Many people will find their land conditioning easier to fit in than their water work, because the facilities for it are constantly available.

Of the three facets, flexibility and strength are the most important. Most general and local endurance can be obtained, after all, by actually rehearsing the movement in water. However, a little early season running or circuit training should do no harm, and will provide variety as well as a useful way of building up the cardiovascular system. However, running will also have the effect of tightening up the leg muscles, so it should only be done when you can also do some loosening work.

Strength is important in the water. Whole power (which can be identified as strength $\times$ speed of muscular movement $\div$ time) is very important in the short sprints, strength means being able to sustain that power for a longer period of time, and is important through to 100 metres. Power is more important on the starts and turns. Both power and strength are hard to develop in the water.

Flexibility can be developed by:	Strength can be developed by:	Power can be developed by:
Biokinetic swim bench (some endurance)	Ballistic stretching exercises	Nautilus – maximal lifts
Mini gym (pulley) (some endurance)	Passive stretching exercises	Weight training
Nautilus – lower repetitions	Partner work in stretching	
Weight training		
Isokinetic exercises		

When a swimmer pulls himself through the water, he has a considerable amount of drag to overcome, and the amount of force he generates relates directly to this.

Someone who weighs more should be able to generate more power if his weight/strength ratio is high enough. You can test leg power either by a standing broad jump or by a vertical jump. Power can be developed by improving strength.

One of the best ways of building strength is isokinetic exercise. It has certainly proved to be more effective than weight training, or even nautilus work. Through isokinetic exercise, power can be developed because isokinetics work on the speed of muscular movement. Isokinetics allow the muscles to work at their maximum through a full range of movement even at fast speed. The muscles work to their maximum force, whether they are slow or fast twitch fibres.

The other great advantage is that the exercise carried out is specific to swimming (see illustrations in following pages) and specific strength is vital.

Not much is known about the optimal intensity, frequency and duration of power training. For swimmers the problem is how best to simulate the conditions of speed, i.e. what actually happens when power is used in the first 50 or in a 50 metre race. What probably comes closest is an exercise consisting of 35 seconds of repeated contractions. The difficulty in swimming lies in achieving this without putting on so much bulk that it increases drag and makes the swimmer too inflexible.

Strength training
Weight training these days is split into categories – free weights, which would include use of dumbells and barbells; and the universal gym type of weight training, where the weights are fixed. Most sports halls use the latter, because the risk of injury is reduced. Weights of this type can be pegged so that, if the body can't control them they don't drop down too far. Many of the exercises with this type of all-embracing equipment simulate the exercises with the free weights but under a controlled environment.

In setting your own weights, you need to be specific in the exercise you set and at the same time produce a well rounded session which exercises all parts of the body.

Land Conditioning Exercises

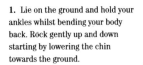

1. Lie on the ground and hold your ankles whilst bending your body back. Rock gently up and down starting by lowering the chin towards the ground.

2. Place the sole of one foot on the inside of the opposite upper leg. Holding the ankle of the outstretched leg, bend at the hips and lower the nose to touch that leg.
3. Repeat with leg turned out.

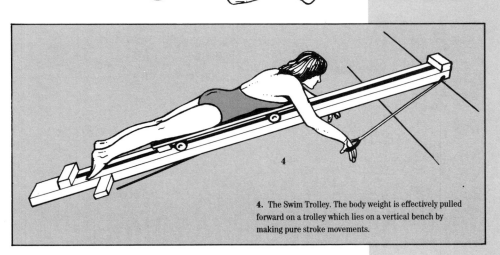

4. The Swim Trolley. The body weight is effectively pulled forward on a trolley which lies on a vertical bench by making pure stroke movements.

5. Kneel on the floor. Arch backwards with either the arms placed on the ground at your sides (i.e. with the elbows on the floor) or with the hands behind the head. The arching movement is brought about by looking back over the head.

6. The Crab. Lie on the ground and place the hands so that the elbows are bent and the fingers point back towards the feet whilst positioned over the ears. Push down with both feet and hands to straighten the arms and legs.
7. Kneel on the floor, whilst holding the ankles, look back over the head and arch the back as far as possible.

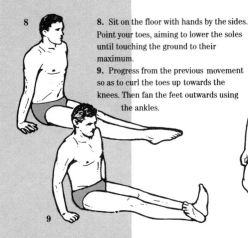

8. Sit on the floor with hands by the sides. Point your toes, aiming to lower the soles until touching the ground to their maximum.

9. Progress from the previous movement so as to curl the toes up towards the knees. Then fan the feet outwards using the ankles.

10. Whilst standing, turn the feet outwards so that the heels are adjacent to one another. The feet need to be in a perfect straight line, with the knees out. The knees are then bent as far as possible.

11. The swimmer squats with hands placed on the ground out in front, keeping the back straight. He stretches one leg out to the side, leaning on hands, then bend the knee on the outstretched leg and change legs.

12. Single arm circles, rotating one arm through 360° in a circle closer to the head can be followed by alternating arms with one arm going in one direction and the other arm in the other direction.

14. Place one hand behind the back and reach towards the other hand which is bent back behind the head. When the fingers finally interlock, pull hands towards one another.

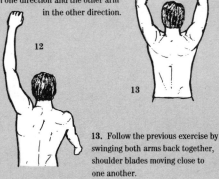

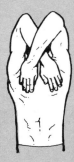

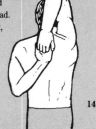

13. Follow the previous exercise by swinging both arms back together, shoulder blades moving close to one another.

15. Bend the elbows and place the palms of the hands on the shoulder blades so that they cross at the forearms. Attempt to reach down the back as far as possible.

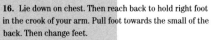

18. Kneel on the ground. Lower the head and attempt to touch the ground in front of the head with clasped hands and the forearms.

16. Lie down on chest. Then reach back to hold right foot in the crook of your arm. Pull foot towards the small of the back. Then change feet.

17. Whilst kneeling on the floor, throw hands in semi circular sweep over head. Then, rock back on feet so that feet roll back over balls of toes.

68

19. Kneel on the floor and place your hands on the back of your head. A partner, who is standing behind you, aims to gently pull your elbows together.

20. Remain kneeling on the floor. Place one hand on the shoulder blades by reaching behind your head. Press steadily on your elbow whilst aiming to get the fingers of your hand as far down your back as possible.

21. Kneel on the ground with your feet splayed sideways. With balancing your body on the ground, your hands look back over your head and arch the back as much as possible.

22. Lay flat on the ground. Place your hands on the ground by your sides. Press down with your hands and arch your back as much as possible.

23. Two variations on the previous exercise are one with the arms placed behind the head, and the other with your hands clasped behind the small of the back.

24. Whilst standing, arch your back and rotate from side to side with the elbows bent. Attempt to arch your back as much as possible in order to increase the degree of difficulty.

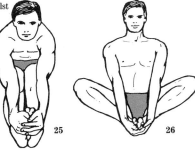

25. Sit on the floor and whilst curling the body as far as possible, attempt to wrap your hands around the bottom of your feet.

26. Sit on the floor with knees out, hands clasped around feet and with shoulders well back.

27. From this stretched position, curl the body and aim to place your forehead on your feet.

28. Whilst sitting and facing a partner, hold your partner's ankle and turn the toes through 180° by placing gentle pressure on the toes.

29. Sit on the ground with the toes relaxed. Keeping the heels on the ground, curl the toes in to touch one another.

30. Using a partner, lie face down. Bend your elbow. Your partner places gradual and steady pressure on your elbow so as to press the elbow through a perpendicular position, towards your head.

31. Whilst sitting, hook a towel over your feet. Rock backwards over the buttocks trying to create as large an arc with the feet as possible.

32. Hook a towel around the front of your ankles. Pull the sole of your foot up towards the small of your back.

33. Kneel and spread your arms and hands out wide with your fingers spreadangled. Keeping the chin forward and the kneeling posture, arch your back as far as you can.

34. Hold a towel in both hands behind the back. With your back straight and both hands still holding the towel, swing the towel through 180° until the towel is in front of the body.

35. Whilst standing, try to get the hands to touch behind your back whilst keeping the arms in line with the shoulder.

36. Lie on the ground, face downwards. A partner then holds the ankles and gradually presses the feet either side of the hips.

37. Lie in the same position but on this occasion, your partner aims to place the soles of your feet against the small of your back.

70

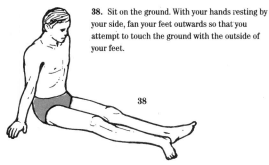

38. Sit on the ground. With your hands resting by your side, fan your feet outwards so that you attempt to touch the ground with the outside of your feet.

38

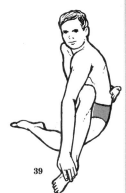

40

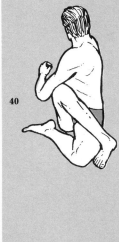

39. Sit on the floor with one leg in front of your body and the other bent underneath the arch created. Aim to place one arm straight along the line of the front leg and bend the elbow so as to place the other arm behind the back by bending at the elbow. Alternate arms and legs.

40. Then, attempt to turn the head so that the elbow is placed behind the front knee and the chest faces behind.

39

A good exercise warm-up which increases the heart rate is paramount. An injury could set your training programme back weeks. Approach your weight training sensibly by following the correct technical rules. The simplified version of these rules is:

1 Breathe naturally.

2 Keep chin high, bend knees and keep back straight when lifting from ground.

3 Try to build up weight gradually.

4 Keep your back straight when pressing weights above head.

5 Control weights up and down without jerking.

6 Use a mirror at first if you can position one suitably.

The universal types of equipment make it very difficult either to injure yourself or to lift incorrectly.

The first three to four weeks of your weight programme should be endurance orientated in order to build up correct technique and muscular efficiency in the various movements. Normally 20 to 30 repetitions should be sufficient.

Strength can best be obtained through a pyramid of lifting; for example, 10 repetitions, rest, 6 repetitions, rest, 3, rest, 2, rest, 1. Each time, the weight is increased. High repetitions (e.g. 3×10) only increase muscular endurance, rather than strength.

41. Bend forward, placing both hands on the wall with heels on the ground. This action stretches the muscles at the back of the leg. The arms need to be at full stretch and, if this isn't achieved, you should stand further back.

42. Stand on the floor. Clasp the hands together behind the buttocks. Bend forward and attempt to place the backs of the hands on the ground behind the head.

43. Sit on the floor with one foot placed on the inside of the upper leg.

44. With one hand clasping the appropriate ankle, place the chin on the knees. Then change to the other leg.

Anyone who is planning for distance swimming can emphasize the repetitions, whilst the sprinters can work on pyramids. This type of work is known as isotonic training.

Isokinetic training

Isokinetic training has the advantage of being more closely associated with strength because muscles can be put under maximum stress over the full range of motion. Strength gains are more consistent across different joint angles. In addition, the equipment used for isokinetics more closely follows the movement patterns whilst swimming.

Mini gyms, leapers, swim trolleys and swim benches along with other equipment demonstrate this (see photographs in Chapter 5). Here again, there is less likelihood of injury to the swimmer from using a weight at fast speed. With the help of the isokinetic swim bench, one can work on the high elbow recovery and pull necessary in freestyle and butterfly and you can make sure that your hand is moving through the right position under the body (see photograph on p. 85).

The rate of work should be as close to swimming speed as possible if it's to be of

72

value to strength. You can also work on the swim for the approximate length of your own race or event and then rest. You can adjust the level of resistance by setting the machine on certain numbers (e.g. 8 or 9).

There are some more explosive basic exercises which you can use for strength as well as power. These have the added advantage of being easily measurable. You can see distances achieved and this aids motivation. These exercises are:

Standing broad jump This is a standard test of leg strength and relates to power in the leg. The swimmer stands behind a line, bends his knees and swings his arms so as to co-ordinate a forward and upwards drive of the legs with the arm swings. The distance covered in this two-footed jump can then be measured.

Vertical jump Another standard test of strength. The swimmer chalks one of his hands and stands facing a wall with his hand above his head. He bends his knees and then jumps as high as he can. The distance can be measured by the chalk marking on the wall.

Pull ups or chins to a bar The swimmer grasps his hands over a horizontal beam or bar. The arms are extended over his head as his aim is to lift his chin to the bar. There are elements of muscular endurance in this but as the swimmer is moving slowly and carrying his own body weight, arm strength is a major measurable component.

Dips The swimmer stands between two high backed chairs, solidly placed on the floor. Bending his knees he places his hands on the top of the chairs which are placed either side of him. Looking directly ahead of him, he bends his elbows until he forms a right angle at his elbow. Stronger people can perform many repetitions with their own body weight. This is very good for the triceps but has a high element of endurance as well as strength in it.

Arm strength exercises with pulleys

Arm strength can be gained from the use of surgical tubing for pulling. This is attached to a point on a wall or door and the swimmer bends forward and pulls against the tubing with alternating arms in a front crawl action. It is a good idea to pull in a series of repetitions equivalent to the distance over which you intend to swim. You can repeat this with butterfly arm movements. Backstroke arm movements here have to be practised with the body lying prostrate. The backstroke pull is then made from behind the head. Other exercises can be brought in, isolating particular muscle groups. The deltoids are very important muscle areas to build up, because if worked on they will help to prevent tendonitis, and also because they are used in the recovery and pull (see photo).

To isolate the anterior deltoid, place the tubing under the foot whilst standing, with the thumbs facing upwards and the end of the tubing in your right hand, pull the tube until the hand is level with the hips. Try this twenty times with each hand and then drop hands. The middle deltoid can be worked on by carrying out the same movement with the palm of the hand facing down and the thumbs forward. The posterior deltoid, the third part of this muscle belt, can be worked on again in the same way, but this time with the palm facing backwards and the tube being pulled back behind the body in simulation of the end of a front crawl pull.

The accompanying suprispinatus muscle can be strengthened while standing, and whilst holding the tube with the thumbs facing down, the swimmer pulls the tubing down and diagonally back[19]. Rotation of the elbow constantly takes place in swimming. The following exercise can help rotation.

Stand to one side of the end of the tubing. Keep the elbow up against the side of the body and the hand forward, slightly in front of the body. Try to pull the hand across the front of the stomach. The tube should resist the internal rotation of the shoulder. Then change arms. External rotation can be improved by slowly rotating the lower arm in the opposite semi-circle.

Adopting the same position, adduction, another important movement in swimming, can be improved by pulling the tube (whilst the body is standing) across the front of the body four centimetres beneath the line of the hips. Adduction is used for the middle phase of the pull in freestyle and butterfly when the hand is pulled under the body before recovery.

Exercising with surgical tubing can be very useful in building up arm strength. It is best to correlate the benefits to the individual in terms of endurance and strength, but there is little doubt that there is some benefit to be gained in the lumbar region from these types of exercise. They are also a way of slowly rehabilitating the shoulder region after injury.

Flexibility

Before you start and during a flexibility programme, you are going to need to make a regular check on your flexibility. The main areas on which you will be working are in the shoulders and ankles. Hip mobility, which plays some part in rotation, particularly in butterfly, is more difficult to measure. The measurable ranges are:

1 Ankle plantar flexion.

2 Ankle dorsi flexion.

3 Shoulder flexion.

4 Shoulder extension.

5 Inversion of foot and ankles.

6 Eversion of foot and ankles.

Most of this flexibility can be measured with the use of a giant 180° protractor. You can make a simple version yourself by extending the lines from an ordinary protractor on to a large piece of cardboard.

The swimmer sits on the ground, with the feet and lower part of the legs on either side of the vertical cardboard. He plantar-flexes his feet (1) by pointing and pressing his toes towards the ground. The degree to which he can do this will then be measured by the protractor on the cardboard. Using the same procedure, he can measure his ability to dorsi-flex (2) by curling his toes up and measuring in the same way.

Shoulder flexibility is also important, the rotation of the shoulder joint playing a large part in swimming. It's possible to determine shoulder flexion and the extension with the help of a partner. Shoulder extension (4) can be measured by getting the swimmer to stand with his back about a metre from the wall. He then stretches both arms back with the arms straight and in line with his shoulder. The partner marks the points where the little fingers rest. The distance between the little fingers can then be measured and logged.

Shoulder flexion (3) is equally easy to measure. The swimmer lies flat on his face so that his extended arms touch a wall. With the face remaining on the ground (4) and his hands locked together the swimmer lifts his hands as high as possible up the wall. The partner then measures the distance achieved.

In swimming, the ability to *toe in*, i.e. to relax the ankles on the up kick or recovery of the legs, is important. If the ankles are sufficiently flexible, the water can press back on the toes and the range through which the feet can kick is increased. The capacity of the feet to evert and invert therefore becomes important. This can be measured by getting the swimmer to lie on his back with his lower leg over the cardboard protractor. The leg should be lying along the protractor's 90° line, and the heel along the base line.

The swimmer now turns his sole in as far as he can whilst keeping the heel flat on top of the cardboard. The foot inversion (5) can then be measured by the position of the big toe or the centre of the inside of the ankle. Eversion (6) means the opposite. The swimmer aims to turn the foot itself out as far as possible. The lower legs stays fixed on the cardboard at 90°, and the measurement is made so as to determine the amount the little toe curls from the baseline.

With a knowledge of his own flexibility, the swimmer can now build up his own programme so as to work on areas in which he knows he needs to improve. In an earlier chapter, I outlined a few poolside exercises that the swimmer could undertake to improve flexibility. There are many such exercises. I have listed a few in this chapter. Most of them can be used either at the side of the pool or at home, or the local sports hall or gym.

Although there are three known methods of stretching, we need only concern ourselves with the two which bring most benefit to an adult swimmer: *ballistic stretching* and *static stretching*. Static stretching involves forcing a joint beyond its normal range, as in many of the tests for flexibility. By comparison, ballistic stretching is associated with movement and speed, and muscles being moved out of their normal range often in association with work, quick recovery during swimming.

Much of the static stretching requires a partner. The partner should never use force – this could do long-term damage to the whole muscular area.

11 KEEPING RECORDS

Often people don't know how long they are going to train for. Sometimes it could be a matter of doing a few weeks or months and then stopping, only to try again later. The keeping of a log is therefore important as a permanent record of progress and as a means of comparison. The records need to be split into three sections:

1 A medical section, which should be completed after a medical check every six months.

2 A section which records all regular support material. This should be completed every month.

3 A third section which records the daily training sessions. This should be completed after each session.

Your log can either be home-made or purchased from your national swimming association.

Section One

Every six months, a medical check should enable you to log:

Height and weight	Length of limbs lower arm
Pulse rate	upper arm
Diastolic blood pressure	lower leg
Systolic	upper leg

Tests should be made to include:

1 Blood screening (e.g. anaemia)

2 Cardiogram

3 Lung function (via spirogram – e.g. asthma)

4 Urinalysis

Your doctor will need to know:

1 Any drugs being taken.

2 Any history of family illnesses.

3 Any part of your medical history not already known to him.

The log should include any comments by your doctor on general fitness, such as:

1 Assessment of any diseases, either already present or newly diagnosed.

2 Possible health and life style problems having a bearing on performance.

3 Possible musculoskeletal problems which could show up in training.

Section Two

Each month, the following material should be included:

Resting pulse rate   Flexibility levels:

Height
                                 Ankle plantar flexion

                                 Ankle dorsi flexion

Weight   Inversion of feet

                                 Eversion of feet

Subcutaneous fat ratio   Shoulder flexion

                                 Shoulder extension

Best – number of strokes per 25 metres in month at maximum speed.

              number of strokes per 25 metres in month at medium speed.

Target times for month.

Personal best times in month in race.

Personal best times in month in training.

Overall breakdown of

How many training sessions in month.

How much time devoted in month.

How much distance in each month.

where training was completed.

(on a week-by-week basis)

Section Three

Your training logs could be laid out as follows:

Date: **Time:**   **Pool:**

Distance Stroke	No. of repetitions	Rest time	Pulse count	Any outstanding performances

A general training scene in an everyday club coaching situation.

12 THE BIG DAY

Preparing for the big test

This section assumes that your objective is a major competition or a long distance swimming championship. The swimmer will need to determine at the start of the season where he wants his peak to be and then structure his whole season in such a way as to bring it about.

In terms of competition, there needs to be a steady build-up of competitive events towards this pinnacle. Too much competition will ruin the taper, in the month of training leading up to the big day. For most swimmers, the major events usually take place in July or August. A structured season might look like the table opposite.

After months of hard work, the swimmer now needs to rest and sharpen up for the big test. With a month to go, the swimmer starts to:

1 Take longer rests between repetitions.
2 Include more sprints.
3 Reduce the length of swims.
4 Sleep more.
5 Concentrate his mind on the test ahead.
6 Sharpen up his starts and turns.

The period over which this occurs is known as the taper. The main factors affecting the rate of taper are:

1 Your age.
2 Your strength.
3 How much training you have behind you in the past year and your subsequent fitness.
4 The length and type of event you are concentrating on. The taper is very much a matter of personal choice. Some people prefer to rest very little and to

Period	Swimming performance	Mental work	Land conditioning
Sep–Dec early season preparation	1 Over distance work – short rest 400s + 800s 2 Stroke drills 3 Stretch hard swimming	1 Set target times for year 2 Work on goals for training	1 A little early running 2 Heavy weights – pyramids 3 Test own strength + flexibility and measure these 4 Flexibility work
Jan–March overload training pre-competitive period	1 Over distance work increases 2 Starts + turns 3 Kicking + pulling work 4 CIM + cruise sets 5 Develop pace control	1 Self-discipline in training programmes 2 Monitor diet + sleep	1 Heavier weights 2 Mini gym + swim bench 3 Flexibility continues
March–May competitive period	1 Increase in quality work 2 More anaerobic work 3 Reduce distances on CIM work 4 Harder, shorter kicking 5 Negative splits 6 Reducing work	1. Select races 2 Relate training targets to mental approach	1 Further Nautilus work 2 Flexibility 3 Target weights
June–Aug long course season	1 Increase aerobic work 2 Increase sprints 3 More broken swimming 4 High quality and reducing swims 5 Starts + turns	1 Develop race strategy 2 Adopt positive approach 3 Self-motivate towards targets in racing period	1 Slightly less weights – work on pyramids 2 Flexibility 3 Swim bench work – check on position of pull

concentrate on sharpening up at the very last minute.

A strong swimmer who is entering sprint events will need a lot of rest. Many swimmers have had difficulty in getting the taper absolutely right. Often it is a matter of trial and error. There is a very fine line between a good performance and a bad one. Too much rest can make a swimmer unfit. Often distance swimmers and swimmers who recover quickly from training like to have a very short taper – possibly only three or four days, particularly if they taper and retaper over two or three races while working towards a major peak.

Mental effect of taper

The main result of a taper should be one of a mentally and physically rested swimmer who is confident of success. Large drops in time frequently come about as a result.

Many swimmers like to shave their bodies in order to enhance this feeling of well-being before competition. Tapering is as much mental as physical. Having rested up, the swimmer feels better than at any other time in the season.

Physical effect of taper

The swimmer's body works hard throughout the season, and as each piece of training is soaked up, so the body adapts to increasingly hard bouts of training. Every so often, however, the body fails to adapt (post-adaptive phase), and the swimmer becomes stale. During the taper, the swimmer should adapt to training in an optimum manner (super-adaption as it has become known). This type of adaption involves lactate removal and increased enzyme activity. Often this can best be brought about by continuing to overload the body until a week before competition.

The concentration on pace needs to be sustained throughout this period. The middle distance swimmer needs to rehearse negative splitting, i.e. getting used to the idea of swimming the second half of the race as fast as the first. Some swimmers may find this difficult to do. For instance, over 400 metres they may prefer to swim their first 100 in a time approximately six seconds slower than their best 100 metre time; the next two 100 metre swims two seconds slower still, and the last 100 just half a second faster. This could best be rehearsed through broken swimming during the taper. An example of the times might look like this:

100 metres freestyle –	best time – 1:02.0	
Target 400 freestyle –	1st 100 – 1:08.0 2nd 100 – 1:10.0 3rd 100 – 1:10.0 4th 100 – 1:09.5	 Time 4:37.5
Broken swim in training –	1st 100 – 1:10.0 15 sec. rest 2nd 100 – 1:12.0 15 sec. rest 3rd 100 – 1:12.0 15 sec. rest 4th 100 – 1:11.0	 Time 4:45.0

Try to avoid over-sprinting during the taper. This will deplete the nervous system to too great an extent.

Some basics

You don't want to feel tired on the day of the event, so a reasonable night's sleep is important. Although there is no scientific basis for this, sleep before midnight seems to have more value than sleep afterwards. A lie-in in the morning will also help you to rest up. On the other hand, getting to bed *too* early on an evening when you feel tense will be of little value if you can't sleep.

The right approach to meals has already been related in an earlier chapter, but large fatty breakfasts should be avoided. You should have planned your day on the preceding day. Everything needs to be done in an unhurried way. An easy stroll in the morning with some light stretching exercises will help. Don't over-exercise at this point. Make sure that you get to the pool in plenty of time for your competition.

Strategy

During the morning you should find time to determine your race strategy. If you have a number of events involving heats and finals, you will need to determine which are the key races and how fast you will need to swim in order to make the finals.

Good strategy can create faster or slower times, and the object of it is to win races. As the level of competition improves, so race strategy becomes more important. I like to distinguish between general and specific strategies. General strategies involve factors that most swimmers should consider in their races, irrespective of whom they are competing against. For instance, 800 and 1,500 metre swimmers need to concentrate on either trying to pull away from or catch their nearest positional competitor. 200 metre swimmers need to bounce off the wall at 100 metres, having up to that point concentrated on feeling easy and fresh. They then need to wind up their speed over the next 100 metres.

Specific strategies are tailored to suit individual race situations. They depend on elements of surprise when swimming against other competitors of similar speeds. We all know of many situations where the race favourite doesn't win. This comes about for many reasons, one of the main ones being that the favourite has been put under unexpected pressure.

Going out fast can help break down competitors who are known to finish fast; whereas, against competitors who are known to go out fast and finish slow, slowing the pace down early on can help during the final kick if you enter the last part of the race level. Be cautious when trying to sprint away from other swimmers in the middle of a race. It might be a useful tactic against someone who is easily demoralized, but you have to be confident that this tactic will be successful, because it can take so much out of your body during a race. The application of a relatively sudden but steady increase of pace in an outside lane can be equally effective if the swimmers in the middle of the pool can't see you. You will need to work out which strategy is going to be beneficial to you on a particular day. This will need to be done in advance and updated at the event in the light of who is taking part in a particular race.

The general and psychological approach towards strategy on race day should be

84

one in which you are looking forward to the races, not one in which you are fearful of implementing a particular tactic.

Warm-up

Competitors are often limited in their warm-up by outside factors such as whether the pool is crowded with other competitors, how much time and space has been allocated for each team and group, and whether sprint lanes or starting and turning areas have been made available.

You should warm up for at least twenty minutes, preferably thirty minutes, as near as you can to the start of your race. The warm-up should consist of plenty of easy swimming on a range of strokes, starts and turns and a little short sprinting, mainly over 25 metres – don't over-sprint. Get used to the turning walls by rehearsing starts and turns and, if you are a backstroker, get used to the position of the flags so that you can count the number of strokes to the wall without looking back.

Fartlek swims can help you feel strong in the water. The main object of the warm-up is to raise the pulse rate, and to open up the blood vessels in the muscles which will be employed in the race. These muscles need to be warmed up. Avoid hard kicking. Kick lengths at a moderate tempo during the warm-up.

The other main value of the warm-up is in rehearsing the movement and, as a result, stretching the muscles and loosening connective tissue.

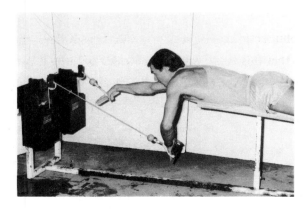

The isometric swim bench. The swimmer lies flat and carries out alternating pulling movements of the front crawl. A metre can be set at the end of each pulley to decrease or increase the level of resistance to be encountered. The pulleys allow the swimmer to push right through towards the hips. Each of the pulleys and metre units can be removed from the swim bench unit and used in isolation as a mini gym.

Your total warm-up programme might well be constructed as follows:

5–10 minutes	shoulder and ankle stretching exercises
10 minutes	easy, long swim which intermittently gets harder
5 minutes	short sprint and starts work
5 minutes	single lengths at medium speed, working on pace and stroke length
5 minutes	turning, and then loosen down

Pre-race activity

The last few minutes before your race are crucial, because everything that you've achieved during the season can be damaged during these minutes.

After you've warmed up in the pool, keep your body warm by having a hot shower and then by putting on your tracksuit. Heat can be lost through your feet, and you will need to wear training shoes to avoid this. Wear additional sweaters if competing outdoors and if a tracksuit is insufficient. Keep your tracksuit on as long as possible.

Remember to keep an eye on the event programme, so that you report and check in well in time for the race. You also need to check basic things such as your goggle and costume straps. Try to avoid competitive verbal interchange with your rivals before racing. You need to build up for the big race at exactly the right moment. This can be achieved by swimming your race through in your mind as you sit on the competitors' seats, immediately prior to swimming the race.

Other factors

Massage and a rub can help before you compete if you believe in it as a competitive tool. It can help to raise muscle temperature and increase flexibility through limb manipulation. Many swimmers also like to hyperventilate before they compete. Hyperventilation consists of taking long deep breaths prior to racing. It can lead to a feeling of dizziness if done too much. It has the advantage of reducing carbon dioxide content in the blood. Three or four inhalations should be sufficient; beyond that the oxygen intake is of little value.

Long distance or marathon swimming

The most important aspects of preparation for long distance swimming are mental training, physical conditioning and logistical planning. Physically one has to be capable of coping not only with the distances set but also with cold temperatures and currents. If you are unable to cope with all this, then you will need to lower your goals. In your mental approach, you will need to be confident that you can complete the swim. It's also extremely important to have a helpful crew who can make sure you can navigate the course correctly. There will be many unpredictable elements, and success or failure is dependent on the swimmer's ability to cope with these as much as to swim.

Your coach and navigator will need to work together to produce the safest and shortest course, and in co-ordinating the support boat and activities. If the water or weather conditions change, they must know how to react quickly, particularly if you are nervous.

Nourishment at the start and greasing down before you take part is important. Then you can concentrate on the swim itself. You also need to have a knowledge of water conditions and wind patterns. Local knowledge is important, which means carrying out research before you start.

For the marathon swimmer, therefore, there are a number of special factors to be aware of in addition to the normal preparation for racing.

APPENDIX

Information sources

For information about your nearest swimming pool or class:

The Institute of Baths
Management and Recreation
Management,
Giffard House,
36-38 Sherrard St,
Melton Mowbray,
Leics. LE13 1XJ.
(Tel. 0664 65531)

The National Sports Council for
Wales,
Sophia Gardens,
Cardiff CF1 9SW.
(Tel. 0222 397571)

The Sports Council,
16 Upper Woburn Place,
London WC1 0QP.
(Tel. 01 388 1277)

The National Sports Council for
Scotland,
1 St Colme St,
Edinburgh EH3 6AA.
(Tel. 031 225 8411)

The National Sports Council for
Northern Ireland,
House of Sport,
Upper Malone Rd,
Belfast BT9 5LA.
(Tel. 0232 661222)

For information about training squads, Masters clubs or swimming clubs:

The Amateur Swimming
Association,
Harold Fern House,
Derby Square,
Loughborough,
Leics. LE11 0AL.
(Tel. 0509 230431)

The Scottish Amateur
Swimming Association,
Airthrey Castle Annexe,
University of Stirling,
Bridge of Allan,
Nr. Stirling,
Central, Scotland.
(Tel. 0786 70544)

The Welsh Amateur Swimming
Association,
National Sports Centre for Wales,
Sophia Gardens,
Cardiff CF1 9SW.
(Tel. 0222 397571)

For information about approved swimming teachers or coaches:

The Institute of Swimming
Teachers and Coaches,
Lantern House,
38 Leicester Rd,
Loughborough, Leics. LE11 2AG.
(Tel. 0509 264357)

The British Swimming Coaches
Association,
P. Bush Esq.
c/o International Pool,
Westgate, Leeds, 1.

For information about long distance swimming:

The British Long Distance
Swimming Association,
Sea View,
153 The Avenue,
Kennington,
Oxford
(Tel. 0865 739310)

For information about water safety:

The Royal Society for the
Prevention of Accidents,
Cannon House,
The Priory,
Queensway,
Birmingham B4 6BS.
(Tel. 021 233 2461)

For information about swimming for the disabled:

The British Sports Association
for the Disabled,
Hayward House,
Barnard Crescent,
Aylesbury,
Bucks. HP21 9PP.
(Tel. 0296 27889)

The following books may be helpful:

Competitive Swimming Manual for Coaches and Swimmers,
Dr J. Counsilman (Pelham)

Science of Swimming, Dr J. Counsilman (Pelham)

Swimming, J. Verrier (via ASA)

Handbook of Swimming,
D. Wilkie & K. Juba (Pelham)

Swimming Faster,
E. Maglischo (Mayfield)

Building a Championship Season, R. Reese (Swimming World)
ASA Handbook (ASA)

Further information on swimming can be obtained through the following magazines:

The Swimming Times,
Harold Fern House,
Derby Sq.,
Loughborough,
Leics. LE11 0AL.
(Tel. 0509 234433)

International Swimmer,
Speedo (Europe) Ltd.,
Ascot Rd,
Nottingham NG8 5AJ.
(Tel. 0602 296131)

Splash-A Channel Four Book,
K. Juba – D. Wilkie
(Hutchinson)

Swimming World,
P.O. Box 45497,
Los Angeles,
California 90045, USA.

Swim Magazine,
via *Swimming World*

Swimming Technique,
via *Swimming World*

Swimming video tapes are available from:

Swimming Video with Mark Tonelli and Duncan Goodhew,
Class Productions,
Freepost BR2737,
Brighton BN2 2SZ.

Swimming Tapes by Don Swartz
via *Swimming World*

REFERENCES

1 O Lippold, MD, *Swimming Times Technical Supplement*, February 1987, p8
2 E Maglischo, *Swimming Faster*, Mayfield Publishing, p441
3 Dr J Aronen, *Swimming World*, April 1985, p43
4 E Maglischo, *Swimming Faster*, p433
5 E Maglischo, *Swimming Faster*, p441-2
6 L Houtkeeper, *Swimming World*, October 1985, p102
7 E Maglischo, *Swimming Faster*, p426
8 Prof I MacDonald, 'Food and Swimmers', *Swimming Times Technical Supplement*, June 1987, p7
9 Prof I MacDonald, *Swimming Times*, July 1986, p8
10 D Dennaugh, 'Supplements in Sports Nutrition', *Swimming Times*, August 1986
11 L Houtkeeper, *Swimming World*, October 1986, p17
12 L Houtkeeper, *Swimming World*, October 1985, p101
13 J Whetton, 'Nutrition for Swimming', *Swimming Times*, March 1985, p33
14 D Bower, *Swimming World*, April 1985, p5
15 *Swimming Times Technical Supplement*, 5 May 1985
16 *Swimming Times*, May 1985, p4
17 *Swimming Times*, May 1985, p4
18 *Swimming World*, April 1985, p57
19 J Aronen 'Swimmer's Shoulder', *Swimming World*, April 1985, p416

INDEX

Aerobic training, 52, 55

Age of swimmers, 2, 5, 20; Masters, 46-7

Alcohol, 6, 38, 38-9; effect on liver/brain, 31

Alternative swims/training, 50

Amateur Swimming Association (ASA), 3, 47, 48; Scientific Committee, 31

Amino-acids, 33, 34

Anaemia, 30, 77

Anaerobic training, 54

Ankles, 20; exercises, 20-3; flexibility, 20-1, 75, 76

Arms, build up of, 14; strength exercises, 73-5

Aronen, Dr J, 28

Backstroke 20; drills, 58

Blood pressure, 7

Bower, Dick, 52, 54

Breast-stroke, 21; drills, 58; injuries, 27

Breast-stroker's knee, 29

Breathing pattern, 54

British Long Distance Swimming Association (BLDSA), 46, 48

Broken swims/training, 51

Butterfly, injuries, 28; drills, 58

Calories, 39; requirements table, 36; expenditure table, 37

Carbohydrate(s), 11, 32, 33, 34; before competition, 42; loading, 44-45; importance of, 40-1

Cardiovascular system, 65

Construction training, 54-6

Controlled interval swimming/ training, 51

Councilman, Dr J., 52, 53

Cramp, 2, 24, 26

Cruise training, 52-3

Dehydration, 39, 42

Descending series/training, 51

Diet, 30, 32-45

Disabled people, 2, 46

Dog paddle, 21

Drugs, cortizone, 26

Ears, 30

Eating, before competition, 41-43; during the event, 43-44

Elbow rotation, 74

Endurance, 5, 29, 33, 42; building of, 49; training, 54, 65, 71

Energy expenditure, 33; needs table, 35

Equipment, 16-8

Eyes, 29-30

Fartlek (speedplay), 50, 85

Fat, 11, 31, 32; levels, 30-31

Fitness, regaining of, 12

Flexibility, 20-2, 66, 75-6; levels, 78

Fluid levels, 42, 43-44

Freestyle injuries, 28

Front crawl, drills, 57-58

Glycogen, 11, 33, 34, 44-45

Great Britain Swimming Federation, 49

Guild of London Baths Managers, 12

Heart rates, 7, 11, 15; during training, 52-53, 57, 67

High quality goal/training, 52

Hip joint, 21; exercises, 23; mobility, 75

Hunt, Dr D., 31

Hyperventilation, 87

Hypoglycaemia, 40-41

Hypoxic training, 54

Ingredients guide, 44

Injuries, 2, avoiding of, 27-31

Isokinetics, 66; training, 72-3

Isotonic, 44; training, 72

Land conditioning, 19-27, 65; table, 63

Legs, building up, 14

Lethargy, 34

Ligaments, 28

Lippold, Olaf, 8

Locomotive swimming/training, 50-51

London Swimarathon, 12-13

Long Course Championship, 59

Long distance swimming, 87

Lung(s), capacity, 7; overloading, 54; working of, 8

MacDonald, Prof I., 34

Maglischo, E., 32

Marathon swimming see Long distance swimming

Message, 31, 87

Masters, 46, 47-48; championship, 48; competition, 3; European and World, 46; Nationals, 59; swimming clubs, 12

Medical checks, 77-8

Mental approach/objectives, 5

Minerals (table), 36

Muscle(s) 74, 80; shoulder region, 27-8, 74; tone, 4; upper leg, 20

Muscular, area/training, 72; endurance, 71; pain, 26, 27-29

National Advisory Committee on Nutrition Education, 38

Oils, 30

Organic fitness, 5

Otitis external, 30

Oxygen consumption, 7-8

Perfect exercise, the 1-2

Phases of the swimming season, 65

Power, 66-7, 73

Proteins, 32, 33

Psychology, 50, 85

Pulse rate, 7, 54, 79, 85; taking of, 15

Race strategy, 84-5; pre-race action, 86; warm-up, 85

Regressive series/training, 51

Repetition swimming/training, 5

Running/jogging, 20

Short Course National Championships, 59

Shoulders, 25, exercises, 25-26; mobility, 75-6

Sleep, before racing, 83

Smoking, 6 , 27, 31, effects of, 31

Speed, 5, development of, 50; race, 54

Speedplay see Fartlek

Sports Council, statistics, 1-2; South East Region, 13

Sprinting, training, 55; short sprinting, 66

Strength, 5, 66, training, 67-72

Stress, 42

Stretching, ballistic, 65, 76; static, 76

Stroke cadence, 13; drills, 57-58

Swim Fit Awards, 47

Swimming Times, 17

Taper, 81, mental effect of, 81, physical effect of, 81-2

Target distance table, 60-62

Timing, training, 56

Tendonitis, 26, 28

Tendons, 28

Training, 14-15, 50-65; aids, 55; construction sessions, 53-4; cruise, 52; high quality goal, 52; hypoxic, 54; keeping a log, 77-82; on your own, 56; planning your season, 59-65; types of training, 55; using weights, 66-71

Vitamins, 37-38, fat-soluble/ water soluble table, 35; requirements table, 35; vegetarians/vegans, 37

Weight, 8-11, Body fat ratios, 10; losing, 10-11; loss, 33; overweight, 8

Wilkie, David, 7

Williams, Prof C., 45